HSC

MAY 1 7 2004

- The… l to choose from. Help!
- What do I do if I have a pretty nice lawn but there are spots where nothing will grow—not even weeds?
- What can I expect to pay a lawn care company? How do I find a reliable one?
- How often should I aerate my lawn? Should I hire someone or can I do it myself?
- Is it true that I have to kill off my old grass before I can start a whole new lawn? How do I do this?
- Should I add straw after I've put down mulch? What about those big pieces of polyester landscape fabric, or lawn blankets?
- How do I protect my newly seeded lawn from marauding birds, especially those seed-stealing sparrows?
- I burned my grass by using too much nitrogen! What do I do?
- Will lawn chemicals harm my pets? Are the more organic approaches to lawn care effective?
- My lawn is full of mushrooms—what am I doing wrong?

## WHAT THE "EXPERTS" MAY *NOT* TELL YOU ABOUT™ GROWING THE PERFECT LAWN . . .

**could wreak havoc with your yard and your wallet!**

In this book, every question you will ever ask about lawn care is answered. Even if you don't have a green thumb, you can still have a picture-perfect green carpet that's a snap to maintain—the lawn of your dreams!

# WHAT THE "EXPERTS" MAY NOT TELL YOU ABOUT . . .

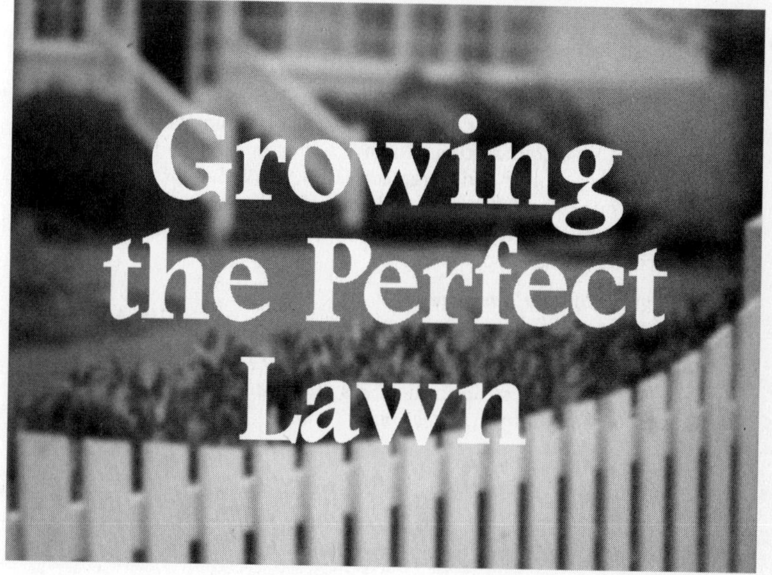


TOM OGREN

WARNER BOOKS

NEW YORK BOSTON

If you purchase this book without a cover you should be aware that this book may have been stolen property and reported as "unsold and destroyed" to the publisher. In such case neither the author nor the publisher has received any payment for this "stripped book."

The techniques and methods contained in this book are the result of the author's experience in working with certain materials. Care should be taken to use the proper materials and tools as advised by the author. It is difficult to insure that all the information given is entirely accurate, and the possibility of error can never be entirely eliminated. This book and the material contained herein have not been examined for safety engineering, consumer and workplace safety, or similar laws or regulations. The publisher will assume no liability for any injury or damage to persons or property that may result from the use or application of any of the contents of this book.

Copyright © 2004 by Tom Ogren
All rights reserved.

The title of the series *What the "Experts" May Not Tell You About* . . . and the related trade dress are trademarks owned by Warner Books and may not be used without permission.

Warner Books

Time Warner Book Group
1271 Avenue of the Americas, New York, NY 10020
Visit our Web site at www.twbookmark.com.

Printed in the United States of America

First Printing: April 2004
10 9 8 7 6 5 4 3 2 1

Library of Congress Cataloging-in-Publication Data

Ogren, Thomas Leo.
What the experts may not tell you about growing the perfect lawn / Tom Ogren.
p. cm.
Includes bibliographical references.
ISBN 0-446-69093-7
1. Lawns. I. Title.
SB433.O4 2004
635.9'647—dc22 2003023825

Book design and typesetting by Stratford Publishing Services
Cover Photo by David Papazian/Corbis

*This book is dedicated*
*to my marvelous wife,*
*Yvonne.*

# Contents

# INTRODUCTION

Summer has always been my favorite time of year. When I was a kid, I could hardly wait for that glorious last day of school and the first day of summer. I'm from a big family (six kids), and many of my oldest and fondest memories are of playing on the big backyard lawn with my brothers, sisters, and friends. Long before such things as Slip'n Slides, we used to put old plastic table covers down on the lawn, put the hose on them, and run and slide. Such fun that was!

It seems as though we went barefoot all summer and never wore much of anything besides swimming trunks. And even today I like walking barefoot across a soft yard. I enjoy the smell of newly cut lawn. I like the way the green grass feels under my feet. Makes me feel so connected to nature, even though I might actually be right in the middle of the city.

There is no doubt in my mind that because my grandparents, and my own parents, liked to plant things—because they liked to have big grassy lawns for us to play on—I have always been drawn to horticulture.

In many ways, I feel I've led a privileged and lucky life. My family wasn't wealthy by any means, but we were a big, loving, fun family and we always had a roof over our heads, food on the table, books on the shelves, and fruit trees, flowers, and lawns. When I was thirty-nine, I took a job as the landscape gardening teacher in a youth prison. I worked there for a dozen years, using gardening as a way to change, to improve, human behavior. It worked, too, exceptionally well. I taught my students how to landscape, how to garden, how to produce and maintain large and lovely lawns.

An odd thing that I quickly noticed teaching in the prison was that many of these tough guys didn't have any idea how to even start or use a power lawn mower. In talking to them, I'd find out that they'd never mowed a lawn, never used a weed whip or an edger, never planted a garden. Most of them had grown up in concrete-covered inner cites, and they didn't know the first thing about lawns.

I believe that nice gardens and lush lawns are something that we as civilized people need to be whole. When I want to relax I just go out in my backyard, sit in a yard chair out on my lawn, and read a book or the newspaper. Sometimes I won't even read anything, I'll just sit out there and enjoy the green, enjoy just being outside. This was the exact sort of thing that had been missing from the lives of my wayward students.

I was mowing my own lawn yesterday, using my push-powered, nonmotorized lawn mower, and was getting a pretty good workout. I have a good power mower, too, but more and more I find I'm really enjoying using the push mower. I may have to pass over a certain spot two or three times to get it mowed right, but still, I get a much better workout—and the lawn always seems to look better afterward, too. But anyhow, I was mowing the lawn and thought about this book. I thought: This is a book for all those people who mow their own lawns. It's a book for the folks who like to know how to do things themselves, who like to know how to do things right.

I confess that it then occurred to me that perhaps it was a little snobby of me to exclude all those people who had their lawns mowed. Some mighty nice people hire gardeners to mow their lawns for them. And no doubt many of these people enjoy and appreciate a neat, nice, lush green lawn as much as anybody. And then, too, just because someone mows your lawn every week, that doesn't exactly make him or her an expert on lawns. Many of these lawn-mowing "gardeners" really don't know the first thing about fertilizing, aerating, topdressing, overseeding, irrigation, and all the other things that go into producing a really top-notch lawn. So even those folks who have their lawns mowed could benefit from an easy-to-understand, fact-filled book on how to have a great lawn.

Terrific lawns don't just happen. A beautiful lawn is the result of caring and doing things right. When you drive through a new neighborhood, you can tell a great deal about it simply by looking at the lawns. People who take pride in their homes almost always take pride in their lawns. And if you keep a handsome lawn out front for all the world to see and enjoy, you deserve to be proud of it. As I said, terrific lawns don't just happen.

So . . . this book is for all of us who remember what it was like to run barefoot across the lawn in summer, for those who missed out on that simple pleasure, and for all of us who appreciate a nice lawn.

But lawns are not just for fun and looks. A good lawn is indeed a thing of beauty, and it adds considerably to the quality of the landscape and to the actual property's value. A healthy lawn is also the safest place for our children to play and where they like to play the most. Our dogs and cats also appreciate a nice lawn. It's an excellent area for trapping rainwater from storms. Rain that falls on a lawn will soak in, not run off into the gutters.

A lush green lawn also has powerful cooling qualities and will save us money as it cuts our cooling costs in the heat of summer. A good lawn is a marvelous thing!

*In his later years, retired at his home at Monticello, our third president, Thomas Jefferson, said, "Although an old man, I am but a young gardener."*

*Good gardeners never stop learning.*

# PART ONE

# An Introduction to Lawns

CHAPTER 1

# Lawns in History

Lawns have been popular for many hundreds of years, and probably nowhere more so than in England. It was in the United Kingdom that the modern lawns first evolved. Centuries ago, there were no lawn mowers to be had; instead, the British nobility employed large numbers of groundskeepers, who mowed their large lawns by hand with sharp scythes. If you've ever tried to cut weeds with a scythe, much less a lawn, you can appreciate how tough it must have been to have a good lawn.

Not all large lawns were hand mown, though. Many were kept in check with a flock of sheep.

Lawns have been big business for a long time. Back in 1613 an Englishman, Gervase Markham, wrote a book called *Way to Get Wealth*. In this book, Mr. Markham described in elaborate detail how to plant, grow, and maintain a green lawn. He claimed that a man could grow wealthy by reading his book and fixing up lawns for the rich folks.

In the 1600s and 1700s, chamomile lawns were quite the rage. Chamomile grows low and stays even lower if kept sheared back. Although chamomile lawns can't handle nearly the foot traffic that a good grass lawn can, William Shakespeare's famous character Falstaff, in *Henry IV: Part I,* said of chamomile: "The more it is trodden on, the faster it grows."

One of the benefits of a chamomile lawn is that the leaves are fragrant when crushed, so it smells good as it is walked on. There are some chamomile lawns here in the United States but they are more popular in England, where the weather is more conducive to their growth. Chamomile does best where the weather is cool but not too cold, where the soil is sandy, and where there's plenty of moisture. Although chamomile lawns smell great when you walk on them, they don't really look like a regular grass lawn, and to some they would probably look kind of weedy.

The green grass lawn as we know it today exploded in popularity in 1830 when Edwin Beard Budding, an engineer from Gloucestershire, England, built the first one-man hand-push lawn mower. By the 1870s, there were dozens of firms manufacturing lawn mowers. Early lawn mowers were nonmotorized push versions and usually had blades on a reel in the front of the mower that worked on the same principle as a scissors. By the 1840s, gangs of reel mowers, linked together, were pulled by horses to mow large estate lawns. Often the gardeners put large leather booties on the horses' hooves to keep them from leaving prints in the lawn.

The first American patent on a reel lawn mower was granted to Amariah Hills on January 12, 1868. Around the turn of the century, James Sumner of Leyden, Lancaster, England, put the first motor on a lawn mower, and by 1902 small, one-man power mowers were being sold in England by the Ransomes, Sims and Jefferies Lawnmower Company. The first electric and rotary lawn mowers were built in the United States in the 1920s but didn't become popular until the 1950s.

Grasses for lawns come from all around the world, and gardeners have long been looking for newer and better species. Our very common Bermuda grass came to America from Africa, perhaps as early as 1593, aboard a slave ship. English settlers brought the hugely popular Kentucky bluegrass from England to Kentucky around 1760. Bluegrass itself has been selected and hybridized so many times that there are many thousands of varieties. Rutgers University alone has produced more than seven thousand kinds of bluegrass.

## Lawns Today

There are those who now claim that lawns are on their way out, but take my advice and don't bet the farm on it. Lawns are part of our heritage and culture and are here to stay.

According to a report from the University of Arkansas, lawn care accounts for more than sixty-one billion dollars' worth of business each year in the United States. This same report notes that there are over five million acres of lawns in the U.S., both residential and commercial. The average lawn today is around three to four thousand square feet in size, and lawns from five to eight thousand square feet in size are considered large.

The average-size lot in a residential area of the United States is around 10,000 square feet, or just under a quarter of an acre (an acre is 43,560 square feet). Sidewalks, buildings, and gardens take up a good part of this square footage. In years past, average lots and average lawns were much larger than they are today. The trend now in residential construction is toward greater density of housing, resulting in smaller lawns.

The statistical U.S. average household is around three people, and if this is divided into the country's population—280 million plus—then there are roughly ninety-three million households in the United States. If roughly 68 percent of these householders own their own homes (U.S. Census), then about sixty-three million households are homeowners. If a dozen average lawns are needed to make up one acre, then it works out that there are indeed around five million acres of lawns in the U.S. just in household lawns. Considering commercial lawns, parks, golf courses, rental house lawns, and so on, then I would assume the five-million-acres-of-lawns estimate from the University of Arkansas to be low. There might well be more than seven million acres of lawns total.

Whatever the exact figures might be, lawn care is definitely big business, and lawns themselves appear to be more popular than ever.

CHAPTER 2

# Species of Grasses

Years ago, there were few choices with lawns. You grew bluegrass in the North and Bermuda grass in the South. But today there are so many possible good choices that matters often get confusing. For example, there are now well over a thousand different cultivars of bluegrass sold. So what's the best choice?

No matter what else, you will want to grow a species of grass that is well adapted to your own geographic area. There would be no point in trying to grow a bluegrass lawn in a hot desert area. It would require huge amounts of water and would die out or look terrible in the midsummer heat. Likewise, there would be no point in trying to grow a Saint Augustine lawn in Minnesota. The first good hard killing frost would also kill off the entire lawn. Lawns need to be made up of grass species that will thrive in those areas. So be sure you get a type of grass sead well suited for your part of the country.

## Buying Grass Seed

After reading this chapter, you may well decide on one particular species of grass for your own lawn. It used to be that you could go to almost any decent nursery and buy a very wide selection of grass seed. But these days, nurseries usually sell prepackaged blends—mixes of different types of grass. In my own area (San Luis Obispo, California), if I want to buy a single species of grass seed, I need to go to a farm supply store to find it. Nurseries or supply yards that sell to landscapers usually will have the freshest lawn seed, and also the most selection.

Sometimes, though, the easiest way to find the exact kind of seed you want is to get it on the Internet. Sources for grass seed are found in the Resources section of this book.

## Seed Mixes

It's usually wise to plant a mix of different types of grass, or at least of different varieties or cultivars of the same species. Lawns that are made up entirely of one kind of grass may look great, but if a disease comes along that affects it, it may wipe out the entire lawn. Having a mix of different but compatible types is insurance against this sort of disaster. It's a good idea to include some grasses in the mix that will tolerate shade, and others that stand up well under foot traffic. Be sure to buy only grasses that are especially well adapted to your own particular area.

### *Insider's Tip*

Check the sale date on any grass seed you buy. Seed should be fresh, and should be sold within a year of harvest. Grass seed is small, and it loses its viability quickly if it sits on the shelf too long.

## Bluegrasses (*Poa* spp.)

The bluegrass category includes all members of the *Poa* species: the Kentucky bluegrasses, the Canada bluegrasses, the Texas bluegrasses, and all the many, many others. For the average gardener it certainly isn't necessary to know all the bluegrass species, so we'll just explore the most common, most interesting, and most useful ones here.

As a rule, bluegrass lawns are highly attractive, fairly easy to maintain, and grow best on clay or loam soils. All types of bluegrasses score very high on "barefoot quality." Compared to other species, most bluegrasses feel exceptionally soft and pleasant under our bare feet. Bluegrass lawns are quick to green up in spring and slow to turn dormant or go brown in winter.

All the bluegrass species will grow best where moisture is abundant. None is especially drought tolerant, and none will thrive where summers are hot, long, and dry. Many are especially cold hardy, however.

All bluegrass lawns benefit from regular applications of fertilizer. As a rule, they are moderate to heavy users of nitrogen. Most species need to be mowed once a week during the growing period.

How high or low to mow will depend on the individual species and cultivars. If you like to keep your lawn mowed short, be sure to pick a particular dwarf grass cultivar that is well suited for this.

All the bluegrasses can be sown from seed or planted as sod. Bluegrass seed is small and often slow to germinate, and because of this it's sometimes sown in a mix with a faster-sprouting "nurse grass," such as annual or perennial ryegrass. The nurse grass sprouts quickly, giving some appearance of a lawn, and it keeps the soil surface shaded until the bluegrass seed sprouts and starts to grow. A blend of perennial rye- and bluegrass will green up quicker in spring than will a pure bluegrass lawn. Creeping red fescue *(Festuca rubra)* grass seed is also often added to bluegrass mixes, since the red fescue grows better in shadier areas than does the bluegrass. When creeping red fescue is added to a grass seed mix, it's normally just blended in at the start, and rarely is there any effort given to getting more of the fescue seed in the shadiest areas. The idea is to have it as a blend.

### POLLEN-FREE BLUEGRASSES?

To date, no one is selling pollen-free bluegrass sod, but in the near future it probably will be available. There are more than a dozen different species of bluegrass that are separate sexed (dioecious), so it's really just a question of time before some smart sod grower selects and starts producing some female (pollen-free) bluegrass sod. The best known of the separate-sexed bluegrass species is Texas bluegrass, *P. arachnifera,* a native species widely grown in the Southeastern states. Texas bluegrass can grow up to three feet tall if not mowed. Mowed regularly, however, it's a very low-pollen-producing lawn.

There is also a newer hybrid cross between Texas bluegrass and Kentucky bluegrass called *P. hybrida* 'Reveille'. This new hybrid works very well in many Texas lawns and is more shade tolerant than either of its parent species, although it grows poorly on soils that are salty or poorly drained.

'Reveille' bluegrass, picking up toughness from its Texas parent, is more drought tolerant than Kentucky bluegrass and will take summer heat in stride.

### KENTUCKY BLUEGRASS *(POA PRATENSIS)*

Kentucky bluegrass is the most commonly and most widely grown of all the lawn grass species. While the species isn't actually native to Kentucky, it is in Kentucky that it grows to its very best, hence the name. Kentucky bluegrass is actually native to Europe and parts of Asia.

Kentucky bluegrass is used as both a lawn grass and as a pasture grass for livestock. There are more than thirty-five million acres of this grass growing in pastures (mostly for cattle and sheep feed) in the Northeastern and North-Central United States. In addition, there are millions of acres of it growing in northern Europe and Canada.

- Kentucky bluegrass is considered a cool-season grass and thrives in many areas where the winters are cold and summer rain is common.
- This is a very long-lived species of grass, and the sod that it makes is considered one of the most barefoot-friendly lawns.

- Kentucky bluegrass is easily the most popular lawn grass in the world. Areas to which it's especially well suited include all of North Carolina, Tennessee, northern Arkansas, and the panhandle sections of Texas and Oklahoma.
- Many people feel that a good Kentucky bluegrass lawn is flat-out beautiful—that it just looks like a lawn ought to look.
- Most Kentucky bluegrass lawns should be mowed weekly in season, and only certain adapted cultivars should be mowed less than two inches tall.

For shady areas, the Kentucky bluegrass cultivars 'Bristol', 'Glade', 'Northstar', 'Nugget', 'Moonlight', and 'Touchdown' are superior. For lawns that will be mowed shorter than the norm for bluegrasses, the cultivars 'Adelphi', 'Bristol', 'Ram I', and 'Touchdown' are best.

### CANADA BLUEGRASS *(POA COMPRESSA)*

Canada bluegrass is a tough, winter-hardy species native to northern areas of Europe.

- Canada bluegrass is long lived, faster to establish than Kentucky bluegrass, and a good choice for stabilizing steep banks.
- This species spreads by underground rhizomes. It will grow on soils that are acidic but also on more alkaline soils.
- Canada bluegrass grows well with less fertilizer than Kentucky bluegrass.
- In northern areas, Canada bluegrass and Kentucky bluegrass are often used in a mix for lawns. The Kentucky species is more attractive, but the Canada bluegrass is tougher and more cold hardy.
- Canada bluegrass, like Kentucky bluegrass, does best on clay or loamy soils, but it will grow on soils too low in fertility for other bluegrass species.
- The best cultivar of Canada bluegrass is probably 'Reubens', which is an attractive and very low-growing lawn seed selec-

tion. 'Reubens' can be mowed lower than other selections of this species.

### ROUGH BLUEGRASS (*POA TRIVIALIS*)

Also known as rough meadow grass, this species is native to Europe and Asia. It has been widely planted in North America for many years and now grows wild over a very extensive area. Although it's called "rough," *P. trivialis* is actually an attractive and fine-textured lawn grass. It's often used in a seed mix with Canada bluegrass or with Kentucky bluegrass.

- Rough bluegrass is more cold hardy than Kentucky bluegrass but not as hardy as Canada bluegrass.
- It grows similarly to Kentucky bluegrass but doesn't have the same deep blue-green color.
- Rough bluegrass adapts better to shadier areas and also to wetter soils than most other species of bluegrass.
- With very little drought tolerance, rough bluegrass will not thrive unless it's growing in soil that is constantly moist.
- It will grow well even where the drainage is poor.
- Rough bluegrass is often used in Southern and Western areas to overseed Bermuda grass lawns during winter months. Where summers are hot, rough bluegrass acts as an annual plant and dies out during the heat of summer.

Some of the best seed cultivars of rough bluegrass are 'Sabre', 'Laser', 'Cypress', 'Sabre II', and 'Colt'.

### SUPINA BLUEGRASS (*POA SUPINA*)

This cool-season bluegrass is native to Europe and has only recently been introduced in the United States. Supina is well adapted for seedling mixes for areas that will get heavy foot traffic. Supina has many good qualities: It's tough, attractive, grows well in cold weather, stays green long into the season, and stands up better than most bluegrass species under constant wear. It has now been used successfully in much of northern Europe and the U.S. and is an excellent addition to mixes of other types of bluegrass, as well as to perennial ryegrass lawn seed mixes.

- Supina seed is considerably more expensive than most other bluegrass seed, but is worth the extra expense.
- Supina can be mowed lower than other bluegrasses. It grows better in the shade than most species.
- Supina bluegrass is not drought tolerant and needs regular irrigation to thrive.
- Supina bluegrass doesn't have that deep blue-green color of the Kentucky bluegrasses, and for this reason is more attractive if blended with Kentucky bluegrass seed.
- Supina seed is slow to establish, and will fill in better when used with a nurse grass of either perennial ryegrass or red fescue.

## DISEASES OF BLUEGRASS

The main, or worst disease of bluegrass lawns is called summer patch. It's a fungal disease and is difficult to control with fungicides. Summer patch usually shows up as dead or dying patches of lawn, often several feet in diameter. Sometimes there will be smaller patches of healthy grass growing within the summer patch lawn.

Summer patch seems to be more common when lawns are fertilized with urea or nitrate fertilizers (see chapter 4), and less common when ammonium sulfate is used as the main source of nitrogen. Also, summer patch is more common on lawns that are sprinkled often, but not deeply. Water less often and soak your lawns to avoid summer patch.

Perhaps the smartest way to avoid summer patch in bluegrass is to plant the right kind of seed in the first place. Certain bluegrass varieties are susceptible to summer patch, and you should avoid planting these. They are: 'Argyle', 'Cardiff', 'Chelsea', 'Chateau', 'Donna', 'Ginger', 'Greenley', 'Kenblue', 'Miranda', 'Nobelesse', 'Park', and 'South Dakota Certified'.

Many of the newer types, sold as "improved Kentucky bluegrasses," are highly disease resistant and are to be recommended. Some of the most insect- and disease-resistant types of bluegrass are 'Touchdown', 'Parade', and 'Merion'.

## Fescue Grasses (*Festuca* spp.)

In the past, fescue grasses were not very popular because of their coarse appearance. These days, however, there are a great many newer varieties, and many of them make excellent, beautiful lawns. Fescue lawns are considered cool-season lawns, but you'll see plenty of them in Southern areas where it's anything but cool. In the very hottest inland valleys, though, fescue lawns do not thrive in the heat of summer. In coastal areas, especially in the West, fescue lawns are quickly becoming the number one choice.

### *Potential Pitfall*

Most fescue lawn grasses can make animals that eat them sick. If you have a dog that always eats the grass, and you have a fescue lawn, you could well have a problem. People who use lawn-type fescue grass in pastures will have problems with cattle, sheep, or horses that feed on it. Some fescue grasses are high in what are called endophytes, and all of these can make animals that eat them sick. There are certain low-endophyte fescue seed blends sold for pastures; these are the only safe kind.

### *Insider's Tip*

With most species of lawn grasses, it makes good sense to use a mulching mower and leave the clippings on the lawn as fertilizer. Fescue grass, though, is very slow to decompose. Fescue clippings left on the lawn will contribute to thatch. With fescue lawns, always rake up or bag your clippings. Don't leave them on the newly mowed lawn.

Tall fescue varieties are the ones used most commonly for lawns. Often these are mixes, and you'll often find other types of fescue grasses in the mixes as well. A great many sod farms now grow tall fescue sod, and over the years the prices for this sod have become quite reasonable. In general, the taller, rougher-bladed fescue sods are tougher and will take more foot traffic than the more dwarf varieties.

### GROWING FESCUES

Most fescue lawns need some extra seed added to any thin spots now and then, a practice called overseeding. This is particularly true of the species grouped as tall fescues. Overseeding involves sprinkling some extra grass seed on the existing lawn. More seed is used in areas where the grass is the thinnest. It's a good idea to mow your lawn lower than usual just before you overseed it. For tall fescue-mix lawns, I like to use two to three pounds of grass seed to overseed an area of about a thousand square feet (twenty feet wide by fifty feet long). If the grass is getting especially thin, I double the amount of seed used.

### TALL FESCUES (*FESTUCA ELATIOR*)

Also called alta fescues, these lawn grasses are quickly increasing in popularity thanks mostly to their easy-to-grow qualities. As a rule they're fairly low maintenance and require somewhat less care—including less water and fertilizer—than most other lawn species. In mild-winter areas, fescue lawns will stay green all year long, and this is their main claim to popularity. They're also long lived.

- While most types of fescue grasses will grow well on heavy clay soils, they aren't well adapted to lighter, sandy soils.
- Usually, but not always, fescue lawns create less thatch than other lawns.
- Fescue lawns are popular for athletic fields and other areas of high use, because they're considered tough and tolerate foot traffic better than most other cool-season lawns.

- Tall fescue lawns are fairly stiff and not especially pleasant to walk on barefoot. For "barefoot-ability," they are not nearly as nice as bluegrass—but still much easier on the toes than zoysia grass lawns.

Because tall fescues are clumping-type grasses and don't spread the way many other types of grass do, to get a nice thick lawn there must be plenty of these little clumps of grass growing side by side. When fescue lawns get thin in spots, it's always necessary to reseed the thin areas with more fescue seed. Actually, it's a good idea to overseed any kind of fescue lawn with additional fescue seed every year.

To overseed, mow low, sprinkle on a thin application of granular fertilizer, and cover the new seed with a thin layer (a quarter inch) of steer manure. Keep the manure moist until the new seed is up and growing. This will keep the lawns nice and thick.

The standard tall fescue lawn variety is called 'Kentucky 31'. It's well adapted to many transitional areas where it gets too cold in winter for zoysia, Bermuda, or Saint Augustine grasses, but too warm in summer for best growth of the bluegrasses. In areas where it regularly gets much below ten degrees Fahrenheit each winter, tall fescue lawns are prone to winterkill. In these areas, bluegrass would be a better choice. In addition to 'Kentucky 31', 'Duster', 'Virtue', and 'Plantation' are all new, improved tall fescue seed varieties. Another very interesting new tall fescue variety is 'Matador', which has a finer leaf and increased disease and wear tolerance.

### FINE FESCUES (*FESTUCA* SPP.)

The most important fine fescue species is red fescue, *F. rubra,* often sold as creeping red fescue.

- Red fescue has better-than-normal tolerance of shade, though it will also grow perfectly well in a sunny lawn.
- It's generally used in mixes, especially for lawns that have shade trees growing in them.

- Red fescue is finer-leafed than the tall fescues, and as a result it's easier on bare feet.
- Like tall fescue, the fine fescues are not especially cold hardy, and are likely to die out in cold-winter areas.
- Red fescue is not tolerant of wet soils and will not thrive in lawns that stay saturated for long periods of time.
- Red fescue does not need high fertilization—nor will it thrive under high rates of fertilizing.

Red fescue is not an aggressive grass, and it's often used in mild-winter areas to overseed dormant Bermuda grass lawns. Red fescue seed is more expensive than the normally used annual ryegrass seed, but the fescue is more attractive, finer-bladed, and will take more foot traffic than will the annual ryegrasses.

'Pernille' and 'Boreal' are the two most commonly used red fescues, although a new seed variety, 'Flyer', has increased disease resistance and will tolerate even denser shade.

### SHEEP FESCUES *(FESTUCA OVINA)*

The sheep fescues species are much more winter hardy than other species of fescue grass. Low growing, fine bladed, blue-green in color, they're not well adapted to heavy foot traffic or to fertilization, irrigation, and regular mowing. Sheep fescue is best suited for large areas that are not maintained as normal lawns. The most useful varieties are 'Quatro', 'Clio', and 'Bighorn'.

### HARD FESCUES *(FESTUCA BREVIFOLIA)*

Like the sheep fescues, the hard fescues are more cold hardy than other species of fescue grass. They're excellent for areas that are droughty and cold in winter. Occasionally these grasses are called hard sheep fescues, and they're sometimes included in seed mixes with sheep fescues.

Although these species are called hard, the individual leaf blades aren't especially hard; the lawns are actually easier on the feet than are their tall fescue counterparts.

For areas that will not be regularly mowed, the variety 'Covar' works well. Discovered in its native Turkey, it has exceptional disease resistance and cold tolerance. Another interesting hard fescue is 'Aurora Gold', which is a hybrid cross between sheep fescue and hard fescue. It's tolerant of the herbicide glyphosate (Roundup), and areas planted to this grass can be sprayed annually with the herbicide. This will kill off the weeds but not the grass.

Other improved types of hard fescue grasses are '4001', 'ABT-HF1', 'SRX 3961', 'Defiant', and 'Nordic E'. The highest-rated hard fescue is '4001'.

### CHEWINGS FESCUE *(FESTUCA RUBRA* VAR. *COMMUTATA)*

Chewings fescue is named for the man who discovered and first promoted it, the late George Chewings. A tough, springy grass, it's the sole species used on the grass tennis courts in Wimbledon. Much of the Chewings seed is grown in New Zealand, where the grass excels. It's a clumping sod grass, useful in particular for shady areas—in fact, it grows better in light shade than in full sun.

- Chewings fescue lawns are not as nice underfoot as bluegrass or bentgrass, but still, they're superior in this to tall fescues and zoysia grasses.
- Chewings fescues are best adapted to cool, humid areas and are often combined with bluegrass in seed mixes.
- Like most of the fescue grasses, Chewings fescue lawns do not do well under intense fertilization practices.
- They're intolerant of high summer temperatures and are not recommended for most Southern areas of the United States.
- Chewings fescues are very fine leafed and drought tolerant; they withstand very low mowing. Since they do not creep, they will not overtake Kentucky bluegrass in mixes, nor will they invade golf greens when not desired. As such, pure seedings of Chewings fescue make sense in these areas when adapted.

The highest-rated Chewings fescues are 'Southport', 'Shadow 2', 'Longfellow 2', 'Treazure', 'Brittany', 'Banner 3', and 'Tiffany'.

## Ryegrasses (*Lolium* spp.)

The ryegrasses are broken down into two large groups: annual ryegrass and perennial ryegrass. Both species are native to Europe and to Asia but are now naturalized (growing wild) over much of the Americas. Neither is the same as the rye that's grown for grain, although they are somewhat related. The ryegrasses are best suited to areas of the country where it doesn't get too hot in summer or too cold in winter.

Ryegrasses will tolerate some shade, and in hot-summer areas the perennial ryegrasses sometimes only survive the summer months when they're growing in shady spots. None of the ryegrasses is very drought tolerant. All need regular irrigation to grow well in areas with low summer rainfall.

Ryegrass of all kinds is often blamed for pollen allergies, and indeed, its pollen is quite allergenic. Nonetheless, any ryegrass lawn that is kept mowed regularly will not shed any pollen at all. Occasionally people get allergies just as winter annual ryegrass is being overseeded on their warm-season grass lawns. They assume incorrectly that the allergy is from the ryegrass, but generally it's due to mold spores that may be in the manure or in any other organic mulch used to cover the seed.

### ANNUAL RYEGRASS *(LOLIUM ANNUA)*

Annual ryegrass is commonly added to many grass seed mixtures. It's inexpensive and germinates very fast.

- Annual ryegrass grows well in cool weather but does not tolerate summer heat.
- Annual ryegrass seed is quite large and light. It takes a good amount of this seed to cover well.
- Because annual ryegrass seed is cheap, watch out for prepackaged seed mixes that are low in price, but are actually

mostly made up of annual ryegrass seed. You never want more than 30 percent of the total mix to be made up of annual ryegrass seed. Read the labels!

- Annual ryegrass is often used as a "nurse crop" along with other, more desirable grasses. A nurse crop is usually chosen because it sprouts fast, provides some shade and cover for the main crop, and is short lived. This use of annual rye as a nurse crop is falling out of favor, though, and most turfgrass specialists no longer recommend this practice.

Annual ryegrass is most useful for overseeding dormant warm-weather grasses. Winter lawns of annual rye growing atop dormant Bermuda grass are usually quite attractive—lush and green. They won't take much foot traffic, though, and when the weather warms up, they start to fade away. These winter rye lawns take a good deal of care and are not in the slightest drought tolerant. So why would anyone bother with them? Well, in certain Southern areas, this is the main way to have a really green lawn all winter. In upscale neighborhoods, a lawn that wasn't overseeded with winter rye would look out of place.

### PERENNIAL RYEGRASS *(LOLIUM PERENNE)*

This species is also used to overseed dormant warm-season lawns. Perennial ryegrass is not an especially long-lived lawn grass, and in order to keep a perennial ryegrass lawn looking really sharp, it will usually need to be overseeded each year with additional seed.

Very few grasses will tolerate as much fertilizer as will perennial ryegrass. In some areas (golf courses, mostly), such lawns are fertilized with as much as thirty-five pounds of actual nitrogen per thousand square feet, per year. This means almost 170 pounds of ammonium sulfate fertilizer (21–0–0) per thousand square feet! Of course this would be applied in split doses, but still, it does boggle the mind.

Perennial ryegrasses establish quickly but spread slowly, thus high rates are always used for seeding. These lawns are easy on the feet while young, but as they age they tend to get stiffer and less pleasant to walk on. Still, they're pretty walkable, if not exactly in the bluegrass category of softness.

You'll find standard perennial ryegrasses as well as many improved varieties.

- Two of the most drought-tolerant perennial ryegrass types are 'Palmer' and 'Prelude'.
- Ryegrass types with increased cold tolerance are 'Eton', 'Goalie', 'NK-200' and 'Norlea'.
- Varieties with increased heat tolerance are 'Derby', 'Birdie', 'Palmer', 'Citation', and 'Dasher'.
- For disease resistance, look to 'Manhattan II', 'Palmer', 'Prelude', and 'Delray'.
- The best-looking finer-bladed, deep green types are 'Brightstar SLT', 'Citation Fore', 'Pennfine', 'Manhattan', 'Derby', 'Palmer', 'Manhattan II', 'Delray', and 'Loretta'.
- Dwarf types don't grow as fast or as tall as typical ryegrasses, and they can be mowed much lower. Some of the top-rated types are 'Barclay', 'Bardessa Dwarf', 'Elka Dwarf', 'Dali Dwarf', and 'Delaware Dwarf'. A typical ryegrass lawn should be mowed at between two and three inches in height, but dwarf kinds can be mowed at one inch or even lower and they'll still look good.
- Ryegrasses are often mixed with bluegrasses and especially with fine fescue grasses. The ryegrass in the mix provides greener color earlier in spring and later into winter. In Southern mild-winter areas (zones 8 through 10), ryegrasses will keep the lawn looking green all winter long.

## Centipede Grass *(Eremochloa ophiuroides)*

Centipede grass is perhaps the lowest maintenance of any of the warm-season lawn grasses. Some call it the lazy-man's grass. Centipede grass seed was first brought to the United

States from China in 1918 by a plant explorer, Dr. Meyer. Unfortunately Dr. Meyer was killed by bandits in China, but his suitcases were later found to contain centipede grass seed.

Because it's native to the milder regions of China and to Southeast Asia, centipede grass isn't very cold tolerant; it should only be planted in warmer climates. It's also especially well adapted to acidic, sandy soils and thrives in many areas of Florida.

It spreads by underground stolons, has large-bladed, somewhat rough leaves, and in frost-free areas will stay green all year long. It can be planted with stolons, as sod, or (usually) as pelleted seed. Centipede grass seed is small, so the coated (pelleted) kind is easiest to sow and to germinate.

Centipede lawns have low fertility requirements, and will often get by on one application of a complete fertilizer per year. These lawns can be made to look thicker, darker green, and all-around nicer with more frequent applications of nitrogen, but this increases the risk of lawn injury from both disease and insects.

This lawn is best suited for people who want a lawn but don't feel like doing much to keep it up. Centipede lawns can be mowed low and are often only mowed every other week. Because this grass stays low and grows thick, it can easily choke out most weeds. As a bonus, centipede lawns are fairly drought tolerant and don't require a great deal of irrigation to look good. Centipede lawns might almost sound too good to be true, and in some mild Southeastern areas—especially in acidic, sandy soils with a pH between 5 and 6.5—they are indeed the best choice. Other grasses exist for these areas, however, that have higher maintenance requirements but are, in general, better-looking lawns.

There are no special varieties of selected centipede grasses—or at least if there are, they're rare. Common centipede grass is what's used. Centipede grass is sometimes confused with Saint Augustine grass, but the two are different species. Saint Augustine is a darker green color.

## Tufted Hair Grass *(Deschampsia caespitosa)*

This very attractive, interesting cool-season grass isn't widely used or at all well known to most gardeners or landscapers. It's called hair grass because if it's not mowed, the hairy-looking seed heads are very long lasting and stand up above the thick grass. Hair grass is often used as a no-mow lawn, and in these cases the seed heads are considered part of the attraction.

Unlike most of our lawn grasses, tufted hair grass is a native species, growing in the wild from as far south as California all the way to the Arctic in Alaska. It's a low-growing, clumping perennial grass that can form very thick sod under the right conditions, where summers aren't too hot. It does best in full sun in cold areas and in part shade in hotter areas. Where summers are cool and humid, hair grass thrives and makes an excellent, thick, dark green, attractive lawn.

Use three to four pounds of seed per thousand square feet of lawn. First mowing should be some forty-five to fifty days after seeding. Seeding is best done in spring or early summer.

- The variety 'Barenbrug' is drought-tolerant and deep green.
- The variety 'SR 6000', considered one of the best for lawns, is drought-tolerant and will also grow on wet soils. This cultivar looks a good deal like creeping red fescue but has greater cold hardiness.
- 'Shade Champ' is another tufted hair grass variety that will outperform most other grasses in shady lawns.

Tufted hair grass is a good, tough choice and should excel in many areas. It deserves to be tried by more gardeners.

## Buffalo Grass *(Buchloe dactyloides)*

This interesting grass is native to those areas of the United States where the buffalo used to roam free and wild. Buffalo grass is separate sexed (dioecious), and there are now female cultivars available that are pollen-free. When buying sod or plugs of buffalo grass, always specify these pollenless female clones, since they need less mowing than do their male counterparts.

Buffalo grass spreads by rhizomes (stems that creep on top of the soil) and forms a fairly thick, very low lawn. A warm-season grass, it goes completely dormant with the onset of cold weather. Buffalo grass does well on heavy clay soils, needs little fertilizer, little irrigation, and is especially well adapted for hot-summer, cold-winter areas where other lawn grasses are difficult to grow.

Almost all the charts I've seen note that buffalo grass grows poorly, if at all, in the shade. Yet I have some growing in my own backyard—'Legacy' and '609', both female clones. They seem to tolerate shade just fine. I've also read that buffalo grass won't take any wear and tear, but in my yard it easily outperforms the Bermuda grass.

Buffalo is somewhat slow to establish. I grew mine from plugs planted six inches apart, and they took all summer to fill in. Moreover, weeds can be somewhat of a problem until this species is well established. Some leftover Bermuda grass did get into my stand of buffalo grass, but when the buffalo was solidly dormant it was easy to tell the Bermuda from the buffalo grass. I then spot-sprayed the invading Bermuda grass and eliminated it without killing the buffalo grass.

Buffalo grass works perfectly well as a no-mow lawn or ground cover. I mow my own buffalo grass about once a month with my hand-push reel mower. It's very fine leafed, almost blue in color, quite attractive, and very easy to mow. It demands very little water and even less fertilizer. While it's true that I don't like the long, brown, dormant winter period with this grass, I plan to overseed mine with some annual ryegrass for winter color. I'm told it's perfectly okay to overseed dormant buffalo grass with annual rye.

I like this grass quite a bit, although I'd be the first to admit that it looks different, and it's not for everyone.

### BUFFALO FROM SEED

Buffalo grass grown from seed will have a mix of male and female plants, and there are two problems with this. First, since the lawn will be about 50 percent male plants, and since these bloom while short, the lawn will produce considerable allergenic pollen even if regularly mowed. Second, the male and female plants grow to different heights, so the lawn will never look very smooth, even after it has just been mowed. For these reasons, buffalo grass is best planted from plugs or sod, and it's best to choose a female clone.

### BUFFALO GRASS CULTIVARS

The three best pollen-free female buffalo grass types are 'Prairie' and the aforementioned '609' and 'Legacy'. Of the three, 'Legacy' is the lowest growing and perhaps the most attractive. Legacy has a distinct bluish color to its fine bladed leaves. It has the occasional male flower, although its pollen is sterile. The cultivar '609' is a taller-growing, greener female form; I have never seen it produce any male flower heads.

## Bent Grasses (*Agrostis* spp.)

Bent grasses are very low-growing, mat-forming, and exceptionally fine-textured grasses, the sort you'll often see used on good golf greens. When grown perfectly, a bent grass lawn is hugely attractive—thick, deep green, lush, and absolutely carpetlike in quality. The bent grasses grow to perfection in the Pacific Northwest and other areas where the summers are long, cool, often cloudy, and rainy. They're found in much of Europe, in Canada, and in the New England states.

Of all our lawn grass choices, bent grass is easily the most difficult to grow well, especially where summers are hot and dry. It's also not very tolerant of warm nights. Nonetheless many people do want to grow bent grass simply because it can be so beautiful. It's moderately drought-tolerant but only looks its best with regular irrigation or rain. A high user of fertilizer, bent grass must be fed regularly and often to thrive.

Most bent grasses spread by stolons (underground stems). Occasionally bent grass lawns will be planted vegetatively with stolons instead of seed. Bent grass seed is tiny—eight million seeds to a pound. One pound of seed will be enough to plant a thousand square feet of lawn. Because the seed is so small, it must be covered carefully and not too deeply. Ideally, an eighth of an inch of steer manure will be plenty to cover the seed. The seed germinates quickly, and grass will start showing after about five or six days.

All types of bent grass lawns need frequent and regular mowing. Your best bet is a sharp reel mower that can be set to cut very short. Different cultivars are mowed at different heights, but all are mowed low—often as low as a quarter inch. On many golf putting greens, bent grass is mowed every three days in summer to keep it looking prime. Bent grasses are also thatch formers; they need to be aerated often and occasionally dethatched. A bent grass lawn that is aerated several times a year will build up much less thatch than one that isn't.

Diseases are always a distinct possibility with bent grasses, especially in areas where they are less well suited. A regular preventive program for control of fungal disease is often necessary. Weeds aren't usually a problem, because the lawn is so thick that weeds have difficulty growing in it. Nonetheless, almost any kind of broadleaf or grass species weed will look out of place in bent grass. A regular herbicide program may also be necessary.

In many Southern states, golf courses are shifting over to putting greens of dwarf bluegrasses or hybrid Bermuda grasses instead of the more finicky bent grasses. In Northern areas, though, bent grass rules.

There are more than a hundred species of bent grasses, some native to Asia, Europe, and North America. The common pasture grass grown for cattle feed called redtop is a bent grass, but is not used for lawns.

- Creeping bent grass *(A. stolonifera* var. *palustris)* is a native grass found growing wild in large areas of the northern United States and across much of Canada.

- Another common lawn species, colonial bent grass *(A. tenuis),* is native to Europe. Colonial bent grass isn't as creeping as some others, and because of this it's sometimes used in seed mixtures, usually with bluegrass.
- In Southern areas, the types of bent grass that will do best are 'Seaside', 'Penncross', 'Emerald', 'Penn Links', 'Cato', 'Crenshaw', 'SR1020', and 'Penneagle'.
- 'Emerald', 'Penn Links', 'SR1020', 'Cato', 'Crenshaw', and 'Penneagle' are newer selections of bent grass and have superior wearability and also increased disease tolerance.

## Carpet Grass *(Axonopus affinis)*

Carpet grass is a perennial, low-growing, spreading, coarse-bladed warm-season grass. Saint Augustine grass (discussed below) is often called carpet grass, but although similar, the two are completely different species.

Carpet grass is often used on poor, wet soils where other grasses will not thrive. It will grow on soils that are too acidic for most other grasses (pH 4 through 6), as well as on very light sandy soils where the fertility levels are quite low. Increased fertility, especially nitrogen, will result in a thicker, greener lawn.

Carpet grass is not cold tolerant or winter hardy and its use is restricted in the United States to Southern parts of the country. In many areas of the Tropics and Subtropics, including large parts of South America, Africa, and Australia, carpet grass is an important lawn grass.

It takes about eight pounds of seed to plant a thousand square feet of lawn. Carpet grass lawns can also be established by planting stolons (underground rootlike stems). Aerating carpet grass lawns slows down buildup of thatch. One saving grace of carpet grass is that when grown with care, it can quickly choke out most weeds. That said, it should be mentioned that carpet grass can escape the lawn and become a difficult-to-eradicate weed in flower beds.

There are no selected strains or cultivars of carpet grass.

## Saint Augustine Grass *(Stenotaphrum secundatum)*

Another broadleaf, perennial, warm-season grass that spreads by stolons. Native to Africa, Saint Augustine is very popular in many coastal areas, especially in southern California. Saint Augustine lawns can be found thriving from the Carolinas down to southern Florida, west through southern Texas, and from mid-California to the Mexican border. Saint Augustine lawns are used worldwide in numerous semitropical locales. The species thrives in the heat of summer and does better than does Bermuda grass in coastal areas, though it's somewhat less cold hardy. Saint Augustine lawns are also more tolerant of salty soils than most.

Saint Augustine lawns will stay greener in late fall and will color up quicker in spring than most types of Bermuda grass, but they are inferior to Bermuda grasses for heavy-foot-traffic areas. Although somewhat tolerant of shade, the grass will be less green and thinner in shaded areas.

Saint Augustine must be planted from plugs, sod, sprigs, or stolons. Many people just get stolons from a neighbor's lawn and use them to establish their own. Saint Augustine lawns are easy on bare feet, and the individual blades of grass, while large and somewhat coarse, are not especially stiff or hard.

In general, Saint Augustine is considered an easy lawn to grow. It's tough, can be mowed low, has fairly good wearability, but needs considerable amounts of nitrogen fertilizer and is a heavy user of water.

A well-grown Saint Augustine grass lawn will choke out any weeds but if an herbicide is needed, note that this grass is not tolerant of 2,4-D, the most common broadleaf herbicide used. Only herbicides that clearly state that they are approved for use on Saint Augustine grass should be used. If you keep your lawn fertilized, regularly mowed, and frequently irrigated in warm weather, weeds will not be a problem.

One thing that often is a problem on these lawns is thatch. Some of the worst thatch I've ever seen was on Saint Augustine lawns. It's important that these lawns be aerated, preferably with a power aerator, at least once every two years. If not, thatch will quickly build up, and eventually a dethatching will be in order (see chapter 8). Removing the clippings after mowing will also slow down thatch buildup.

Saint Augustine creates a very thick lawn when grown right, and it naturally will have a slightly springy feel when you walk on it. When it starts to feel downright spongy, however, that's your sign that the thatch is getting out of hand. Because Saint Augustine rarely flowers, it's a low-pollen type of lawn, but if deep thatch is permitted to accumulate, it can harbor considerable mold, which is of course allergenic. Grown right and kept thatched, this makes a good low-allergy lawn.

An unusual feature of Saint Augustine lawns is the almost permanent lines you'll see from mowing. This grass seems to have more "memory" than most, so it's important *not* to mow it in the same direction each time. Sometimes it's wise to mow the entire lawn in one direction and then to remow it from a different direction. Because it's a thick, tough grass, rotary mowers are generally favored. When establishing a Saint Augustine lawn, be sure to avoid any high spots, since these will always get scalped when mowed.

A recent disease known as Saint Augustine Decline (SAD) can affect and often kill off entire Saint Augustine lawns. When SAD arrives, the lawn just starts going downhill; there's nothing you can do about it. However, it is now possible to buy SAD-resistant sprigs and plugs of selected strains. The most resistant to SAD are the cultivars 'Floralawn', 'Raleigh', 'Common', 'Jade', 'Floratine', 'Floratam', and 'Seville'. Of these, the thinnest-bladed Saint Augustine is 'Seville'. Saint Augustine grass is not a good seed producer, and at this time there is no commercial source of seed.

'Floratam' is a sterile, pollen-free type and is also the most tolerant of cinch bugs in the lawn. The most winter-hardy type is 'Texas Common'.

### Insider's Tip

One popular aspect of Saint Augustine lawns is that those annoying biting bugs known as chiggers don't live in them.

## Zoysia Grass *(Zoysia japonica)*

Zoysia took the lawn world by storm in the 1950s and 1960s. Advertisements for the "instant carpet" lawn were to be found in almost all magazines. In many ways zoysia, which is native to Japan and China, is an outstanding and highly unusual lawn. When grown right, it makes an extremely thick, dense, uniform, low-maintenance, weed-free lawn.

Until recently it was only possible to grow a zoysia lawn from plugs, and these often took a year or more to fill in. Now, though, you can buy and establish zoysia from plugs, or as sod, or even from seed. This seed is small—a pound will plant a thousand square feet of lawn.

Zoysia is a warm-season grass with much better winter hardiness than any of the other warm-season grasses except buffalo grass. Like buffalo grass, it goes totally dormant in wintertime, and this is its chief drawback. If zoysia grass stayed green all year, it would no doubt be the most popular grass in the world. But it doesn't, and in winter it will be brown. Also, unlike many other of the lawns that go dormant in cold weather, zoysia is so thick that it's difficult to establish an overseeded winter lawn on it. Mowing the dormant zoysia low enough for overseeding may injure the zoysia. For areas where snow will cover the dormant lawn most of the winter, zoysia is a fine choice. Zoysia lawns are winter hardy to about Chicago, but north of that is pushing things.

Because zoysia grass is so thick and stiff, it doesn't make a very nice grass to run around on barefoot. It looks a lot better than it feels. People with children might well prefer to go with a different species. Also, chiggers will live in zoysia grass—another reason why children aren't all that fond of it.

Zoysia, when grown right, is considered perhaps the toughest of all grasses, and it will take more foot traffic in stride than any other species. Once wear and tear happens, however, zoysia is slower to reestablish itself in the worn areas than is Bermuda grass. Zoysia grass lawns are quite drought tolerant and need less water to look good than most other lawns. Only buffalo grass and blue grama lawns need less water than zoysia.

Zoysia grass is not a particularly heavy feeder and does not require large amounts of fertilizer to grow well. Three to five pounds of actual nitrogen per thousand square feet per year will keep most zoysia lawns looking good.

Zoysia can be mowed very short—from half an inch to one inch in height—but mowing the grass higher in midsummer will increase its strength and aid in winter hardiness.

### VARIETIES OF ZOYSIA

There are numerous kinds of zoysia grass to plant from plugs or sod. 'Meyer' is the old standby, but there are newer cultivars that are more drought tolerant and more disease resistant.

- 'Emerald' is probably the most drought tolerant of all the zoysia cultivars.
- For tolerance of shade, no zoysia is perfect, but 'El Toro', 'Diamond', 'Belaire', and 'Cavalier' are best. 'Meyer' and 'Emerald' have fair tolerance of shade.
- 'Meyer' and 'Emerald' are less disease-resistant than other cultivars of zoysia.
- If you're growing zoysia from seed, 'Companion' seed is comparable to the better vegetative kinds.

## Bermuda Grass *(Cynodon dactylon)*

This grass isn't actually native to Bermuda—it comes originally from Africa and Asia. It's now an important lawn grass in all mild-winter areas worldwide.

Bermuda grass is a perennial, spreading, stolon-forming grass that thrives in heat and goes dormant with the first hard frost in fall. It's grown in warmer areas but does best in the Tropics and Subtropics. Important as a pasture grass for cattle in many areas, Bermuda grass is one of our most common and most useful lawn grasses where adapted.

No type of Bermuda grass lawn will thrive in the shade, although as a weed in your flower beds, Bermuda seems to do okay in shade or full sun. Bermuda grass is indeed highly invasive and it must be kept in check or it will quickly spread into flower beds and ground covers. If Bermuda grass gets established in ground cover, it's next to impossible to remove; often the only suitable thing to do is to kill off the entire mass and start over. One notable exception to this is Bermuda grass in ivy—there are some specific herbicides for this situation.

Although Bermuda grass goes fully dormant in cold weather, it's well suited to overseeding for winter green color. Typically this is done with either annual or perennial ryegrass seed. When the weather warms up in late spring, mowing the lawn very short will tend to kill off the remaining ryegrass and let the Bermuda grass return.

Common Bermuda grass is a frequent-flowering plant, and it will often bloom and release allergenic pollen even if it's mowed once a week. No other common lawn grass will produce as much pollen as common Bermuda.

As a rule, common Bermuda grass is quite disease and insect resistant, and it will be more so if well maintained. There are many interesting Bermuda grass hybrids, all of them somewhat less disease resistant than common Bermuda.

All Bermuda grasses will form thatch, and eventually this can ruin the lawn. Bermuda grass grows well on heavy clay soils, and over time these lawns become compacted; thatch then starts to build up. Coring or aeration, preferably once a year, is a very good idea on all Bermuda grass lawns. If a lawn is aerated often enough, it may never need to be dethatched. Aeration will also encourage stronger root growth and will make for an overall much more attractive lawn.

Bermuda grass is a heavy feeder and should get around eight to ten pounds of actual nitrogen per year on most Western soils. Ideally the fertilizer will be split into two or three applications. Bermuda grass lawns that are not fertilized at least once a year will become weedy. The surest way to keep the Bermuda grass lawn weed-free is to keep it well watered and well fertilized. A properly cared-for lawn of this type will grow so thickly that weeds can't find a spot to take hold.

Under intensive cultivation, mowing twice a week and irrigating deeply several times a week, all summer long, some Bermuda grass lawns can use as much as fifteen to twenty pounds of actual nitrogen per thousand square feet. Occasionally in some high-pH Western soils, soil sulfur can be used to lower soil pH, but this will not be necessary if acid-based fertilizers are used. For Bermuda lawns on Western soils, I prefer to use ammonium sulfate (21–0–0), which is fast acting, high in nitrogen, and also supplies sulfur, which helps acidify the soil.

## *Insider's Tip*

With a common high-nitrogen fertilizer such as ammonium sulfate (21–0–0), a hundred-pound sack will *not* supply one hundred pounds of nitrogen fertilizer. Because it's 21 percent nitrogen, you'll find only around twenty pounds of actual nitrogen in that hundred-pound sack.

Bermuda grass can be bought as seed, sod, or plugs. The seed is small and light; two pounds is enough for a thousand square feet of lawn. Seed should not be sown until soil temperatures are above sixty degrees Fahrenheit, because cool weather will stop seed germination.

### BERMUDA CULTIVARS AND HYBRIDS

Many of the vegetative types of Bermuda grass are sterile and are essentially pollen-free. These must be purchased as plugs or as sod.

There are also now numerous new and very good hybrid kinds of Bermuda grass that can be grown from seed. This seed is considerably more expensive than common Bermuda grass seed, but it is well worth the extra money: The new hybrids grow thicker, lower, are greener, and are all in all noticeably far superior grasses.

- 'Tifgreen' is the standard against which other hybrid Bermuda cultivars are judged.
- 'Tifdwarf', which is highly attractive and extremely low growing, is somewhat less disease and insect resistant than most of the other hybrids.
- 'Tifgreen' and 'Tifway' are two of the most pest-resistant cultivars.
- 'Sahara' and 'Yuma' are two newer seed types that have extremely good heat tolerance and will thrive in desert areas.
- 'Mohawk' and 'Yukon' are two hybrid Bermuda grasses that have better-than-average winter hardiness and will extend north the range of this lawn grass.
- 'Princess 77' is one of the newest, the most expensive, and easily the best of the new hybrid Bermuda grasses from seed. All other types of seed Bermuda will produce some pollen, but 'Princess 77' is almost pollen-free. It is deep green in color, has a very short dormant period, is extremely thick, is very durable, and can be mowed extremely low. Many of the professional groundskeepers for pro football teams in the Southern states are now switching over to 'Princess 77'.

## Bahia Grass *(Paspalum notatum)*

Another interesting warm-season lawn grass, Bahia has undergone great improvements in the past decade. Although in the past it was mostly a weed grass in Saint Augustine and Bermuda grass lawns, it's now being used more and more as the sole grass in the lawn.

Bahia grass is quite drought tolerant, and since it's so salt tolerant, it can even occasionally be watered with straight salt water pumped from the ocean if needed. It's more disease and insect resistant than most of the other more popular warm-season lawn grasses. Native to South America, Bahia grass is gaining in popularity in many parts of Florida and also some areas of southern California.

Bahia grass is somewhat coarse bladed and spreads from rhizomes (large stems that spread under or across the surface of the soil) and stolons (which are similar to rhizomes, except that they grow above the soil line and root as they go). When well established, it will be almost entirely weed-free because it will form such a thick mat of grass. Unlike most warm-season grasses, Bahia grass has good shade tolerance. Although it will grow and thrive on infertile soils, it responds well to applications of nitrogen. Kept well fertilized with adequate nitrogen, it will be a deep green color.

One of the more interesting aspects of Bahia grass is that when it is growing in soil that is inoculated with the nitrogen-fixing soil bacterium *Azotobacter paspali,* it will produce most of its own nitrogen.

On the other hand, Bahia grass seeds constantly, and many folks find the seed heads objectionable. If the lawn is mowed every five days in summer, the seed heads will be less apparent, but not everyone wants to mow every five days! Bahia grass is not tolerant of high-pH soils and will not thrive where the soil pH is much above a neutral 7. Although it thrives on sandy soils, it grows less well on heavy clay soils. Also note that Bahia lawns can build up considerable thatch and need to be aerated frequently.

Barefoot-ability? The seeds of Bahia grass are sticky, and children may not enjoy playing on this lawn as much as on some others. The blades are also stiff, and it's not an especially pleasant lawn to walk on barefoot.

Bahia grass is exceptionally deep rooted and useful for growing on banks that might otherwise erode. It's used in pastures and provides considerable feed value. Cattle that have been feeding on Bahia pasture will pass on viable Bahia grass seed in their manure. Something to consider if you don't want Bahia grass!

Bahia is fairly easy to grow from seed. Sow at a rate of three to four pounds per thousand square feet. The seed takes between ten and thirty days to germinate—less in warm weather and more in cooler. Bahia seed will not germinate when the weather is less than sixty-five degrees Fahrenheit.

There are different kinds of Bahia seeds for different areas. 'Argentine' is considered one of the better types for the most Southern areas. In Northern Bahia grass areas, 'Pensacola' has increased winter hardiness. For all-around quality and appearance, the variety 'Tifton 9' is probably the most attractive. Professor Glen Burton from Florida State University has developed all of the best Bahia grasses.

## Going Native

A grass is considered native if it originated somewhere in the United States. There is, however, some reasonable confusion over the term *native*. For example, buffalo grass is native to the Midwestern U.S., but is it correct to say that it is native to the entire U.S.? In a way, this is a problem with semantics, but still, any species of grass will only grow the very best in those exact areas where it was originally native. Thus, even though buffalo grass is native to the U.S., it really isn't native to, say, Washington State or Hawaii. And it can't be expected to thrive in either of those areas.

There are a number of native grass species that can be quite useful in areas where summers are hot and winters are cold. Often these are planted and just left to grow on their own, being rarely, if ever, mowed. Lawns made from native grasses should never be treated with herbicides; if a dandelion or two grows up, they can be dug by hand or just ignored. Any lawn that is mowed will eventually need some fertilizer, even native grasses.

Best fertilizers for these lawns are organic ones such as manure, blood meal, bonemeal, or soybean meal. At any rate, fertilizer needs for these lawns are low.

Native grasses can be irrigated or not, but if they are to be watered, they should be watered deeply and infrequently. Deep soaking is more effective with native species of grass because they are generally much deeper rooted than non-native lawn grasses.

If you like, you can grow native grasses in a mix and mow them as you would any other lawn—except they should never be mowed short. Of all the native grasses, buffalo grass can be mowed the shortest, down to an inch, but even buffalo grass will grow better if allowed to grow taller.

The most useful of the native grasses for lawns are big bluestem grass, Blue grama grass, buffalo grass, little bluestem grass, and, to a lesser extent, Indian grass and switchgrass.

None of these native grasses will create a lawn that looks as perfect as a carefully tended zoysia grass, bent grass, hybrid Bermuda grass, or Kentucky bluegrass lawn. Still, they're deep rooted, cold tolerant, long lived, and persistent. They're excellent choices for areas where irrigation water is scarce or just too expensive.

Seed for any of these native grass species can be purchased at specialty nurseries or is easily found online. Seed of native species often contains considerable chaff, and germination rates will often be lower than those of more domesticated grass seed. Also, seed from our native species will often germinate unevenly and slowly, so a certain amount of patience is sometimes needed. Occasionally certain types of native seed will benefit from spending a month or two in the refrigerator in what's known as a period of vernalization.

Seed from native species is best planted with a little fertilizer, then mulched with a light coating of well-aged manure or with straw. Because it may be slow to sprout, the seed should be

## *Insider's Tip*

Remember the old rule of thumb in gardening: Seeds of all kinds should generally be planted no deeper than one to four times their own diameter.

covered so that it doesn't start to grow and then dry out. None of this native grass seed is especially large, and because of this the individual seeds should never be planted more than half an inch deep.

Some people will just scatter native seed where they want it to grow and then wait for it to turn into a lawn, but this is a lousy way to try to establish any sod. It's by far better to plant the seed much like any other grass seed, and then irrigate it, shallowly and often, until it sprouts and starts to grow. And even though these are extremely drought-resistant species, if you want a good, thick stand of grass you'll almost certainly need to water the new seedlings several times a week until they're well established.

Once your native grasses have some size to them and are looking much like a real lawn, then you can start to back off on the water. Even at this point, though, you'll want to gradually wean the new lawn off irrigation. By its second season, your native lawn will probably get by just fine on the occasional rain. Still, keep in mind that if you mow it often, you'll have to give the lawn a good soak once in a while for it to look its best.

Probably the most attractive of the native grasses grown as a single species are the newer female cultivars of buffalo grass, but all native grasses can be attractive. In areas where the lawn is going to be pretty well neglected—where mowing will be infrequent and watering rare—it's a good idea to use these native grasses in a mix. If you like, there's no reason that you can't mix in a little fescue seed with your native grasses. The fescue will green up earlier in spring and will stay greener longer in fall than the natives, while in summer when the days are long, hot, and dry, the native grasses will show their stuff. For those who give a fig, using a mix of native species lets you be perfectly politically correct and still have yourself a pretty decent lawn.

# PART TWO
# The Basics

CHAPTER 3

# Watering and Aerating Your Lawn

## Irrigation: Watering Your Lawn

When should you water your lawn? The best answer is: Whenever the lawn needs it. A dry lawn always can use some water.

Where you live, the type of soil you have, the kind of grass in your lawn, the time of year, the local weather conditions—all these factors come into play when figuring out how much and how often to water. Still, there are some things that always make sense:

- When you water the lawn, soak it. Water less often and deeper. This will result in deeper roots and a healthier lawn.
- Water early in the morning if possible. Less water will be wasted through evaporation, and you'll have fewer problems with fungal diseases.
- Since lawn grasses release their pollen between the hours of 3 and 8 AM, soaking the lawn very early in the morning will knock down most of this pollen and take it out of circulation.
- Sandy soils need more frequent irrigation than clay soils.
- In desert areas, in summer, you may need to water lawns deeply twice a week, and less deeply every day during the peak of the heat.
- Stay off a lawn just after it has been watered. Foot traffic on wet lawns will compact the soil.
- Even the most drought-tolerant lawn grasses will look better with regular watering.

- In areas with normal high summer rainfall, where lawn irrigation is almost never practiced, if a long dry period comes in midsummer or fall it's always a good idea to get out the hose and a sprinkler and give the lawn a good soaking.
- In all areas, it's prudent to give all lawns at least one good thorough soaking just prior to the expected first frost in the area. Many lawns will start to go dormant with the first fall frost, and a lawn well supplied with water will always winter over better than a drier lawn would.
- Wind dries out all plants fast. If it's warm and windy, give your lawns some extra water.
- To see how even a job your sprinklers are doing, set empty cups on the lawn, about five feet apart, before you turn on the water. Afterward, check the cups and see if all areas are getting the same amount of water. Often areas that don't grow as well as they should are getting less water than you think.
- Ideally your lawn will get watered enough that the soil will be wet a foot deep under the lawn. Each lawn is different; each will take a different amount of time for this much water to soak in. To avoid runoff with heavy clay soils, you may need to soak the lawn for about thirty minutes, turn off the sprinklers for an hour, and then soak for another thirty minutes. The only way to know for sure how deep you're watering is to dig a foot deep with a shovel or hand trowel on an edge of the lawn, and see how deep you're actually soaking your lawn.
- If mushrooms keep popping up in your lawn, take it as a sign that you're probably watering too much or, more likely, too often. Remove the mushrooms by hand, throw them in the trash can (not the compost heap), and then rethink your present watering schedule.
- Always remember: If you walk on your lawn and the grass stays flat where your footprints are rather than springing quickly back upright, it's probably too dry. Give it some water!

- If you look at your grass and it seems to be getting a bluish or gray color sheen to it, it's again likely too dry. Get out the sprinklers!

### GARDEN HOSES

If there is a perfect garden hose, I've never seen it. I have over the years bought hoses that cost more than a hundred dollars, and others that cost less than five. Truthfully, none of them has been as good as I'd like it to be. You ideally want a hose that won't kink up all the time, one with less "memory." All-rubber hoses are usually the highest quality and will last the longest. Also, buy larger-diameter garden hoses; the half-inch kind are annoying to use. I wouldn't bother to buy a garden hose with less than a five-eighth-inch diameter. I can't think of any I'd especially recommend, though. What I generally do is throw out my old hoses every few years and buy a few new ones.

### LAWN SPRINKLERS

There are dozens of kinds of sprinklers to go on the end of a hose, and one of the best is the oscillating sprinkler. These move back and forth slowly and distribute water more evenly than other types of sprinklers. You can also get a simple, cheap fan-type sprinkler that has two holes on top and sits flat on the lawn; these aren't too bad, really, and they're very easy to use. You will have to keep moving them to get enough overlapping, however.

Rain Bird–type sprinklers have a spike that you stick in the ground, and they can be quite useful for covering large lawns. Note that you will get what you pay for. The very best are made of metal and by the Rain Bird Corporation. There are many cheaper knockoffs, and some work just fine, but only the real Rain Birds will last.

## Sprinkler Systems

If you don't have an underground sprinkler system, at some point you'll probably want to get one. If you can use a shovel and a hacksaw, if you've ever worked with Legos or Lincoln Logs, you can set up your own sprinkler system. In a nutshell, the process involves digging trenches, installing sprinklers, and connecting them with PVC pipe (which is what the trenches are for).

### GETTING STARTED

Buy all your sprinkler-system parts from a dealer who understands these things. Farm supply stores and nurseries where landscapers themselves shop are by far the best places to get your materials. Ask the folks there to help you figure out exactly how many sprinklers you'll need to get good coverage, and how your system should be designed and set up. Have them give you explicit written directions and instructions on every count.

Lay out the design of your sprinkler system on paper before you get started. It's a good idea, in fact, to do this at the store where you're buying your materials. If they can't help you, find a better store!

#### *Insider's Tip*

In areas where it freezes in winter, it's essential that the entire system of plastic pipes underground run downhill. There should be one low point where you can drain the entire system. This is to keep the pipes from bursting with the first hard freeze.

### THE TRENCHES

For large lawns, rent a small power trencher and use this to dig all the trenches you'll need. For smaller areas, buy yourself a trenching shovel that has a long, slim blade built just for digging narrow trenches. Trenches need only be from four to eight inches deep and about three to four inches wide.

## THE SPRINKLERS

The best sprinklers have some way to adjust the amount of water they release. If a special tool is needed for this, make sure you get one. Likewise, in-ground sprinklers that slowly rotate can be adjusted for output, distance, and area covered. A special small tool is usually needed for this, and it should be included free when you buy your sprinklers. Don't lose it!

With low-output-per-minute pop-up rotating sprinklers, each sprinkler puts out only a small amount of water at a time. This means you can put more sprinklers on the same section (usually called a station in irrigation talk). A setup like this is also easier to build. And because the water goes on more gently, it has more time to soak in—thus there's less possible runoff. The only drawback is that you need to run the sprinklers for a longer period of time to get as much water on the lawn as you would with a higher-output mode. These sprinklers cost a bit more, but they're worth it.

How many sprinklers do you need? I like to have up to a dozen on the same three-quarter-inch line. Have the dealer explain this—each kind of sprinkler is different, and each will put out different amounts of water.

But keep this in mind: If you have too many sprinklers on any one line, none of them will get enough water pressure to work correctly. If your lawn is large, then, you may need to irrigate it one station at a time. Each station will be complete in itself and run independently with its own sprinklers. Each will also need its own valve, either manual or automatic. The best manual valves are the brass ball types, which are much less likely to leak than gate valves.

Consider buying a timer clock and putting your new sprinklers on a timer. Look over the timers before you buy one and read the instructions carefully. Buy the one that seems simplest to use.

## THE PVC PIPE

You want the more expensive schedule 40 (white) PVC pipe for all your sprinkler work. The cheaper, thinner pipe won't last.

Also, use three-quarter-inch PVC pipe for everything; the half-inch kind is cheaper, but less effective.

PVC pipe is generally sold in twenty-foot sections. These can be tied in a bundle and strapped over the top of your car or truck. If you've never used PVC pipe before, cut off a small section and make a practice joint with an inexpensive three-quarter-inch SS coupling. (If you don't know what that is, keep reading.)

### THE PVC GLUE AND PRIMER

You'll need both primer and glue. Use the primer first, then the glue. And a few words to the wise: PVC glue sets up fast—it's welded in place in less than a minute! Still, mistakes can be fixed with a hacksaw, some extra PVC pipe, and some fittings. Also, never set an open can of PVC glue in a box of fittings. If it spills, it'll glue all the fittings together; you don't need me to tell you that this is a bad idea. Finally, any PVC glue that gets on your clothes is likely to never, ever come out. Wear old clothes for this job.

### DETOUR: PLUMBING LINGO

Before we go any further, here's a brief explanation of some plumbing terms for neophytes:

- ***Riser.*** A piece that stands upright.
- ***Coupling* (or *fitting*).** A piece used to join two parts together.
- ***Elbow.*** A coupling used to make a corner joint.
- ***Reducer.*** A coupling used to size pipe up or down.
- ***Tee.*** A coupling that has three openings. It's shaped, as you might expect, like the letter *T*.
- ***S.*** This stands for "slip," meaning a coupling that has no threads; it's intended to be glued.
- ***T.*** Standing for "thread," this is a screw-on piece; no glue needed.

- ***SS.*** A slip-slip joint—that is, each side of the coupling is unthreaded.
- ***ST.*** A slip-thread joint—one side is a slip, to be glued, and the other is a threaded fitting.
- ***SST.*** A slip-slip-thread joint.
- ***Male* and *female.*** A male part fits inside a receiving female part.

### THE FITTINGS

Your dealer should be able to tell you what kinds of fittings you need, and how many of each. Buy extra just in case.

The sprinklers you buy will determine what size couplings you need. The bottoms of almost all in-ground sprinklers have a female threaded fit. If your sprinklers have a three-quarter-inch opening on the bottom, then your couplings will need to be ¾ × ¾ × ¾ inch in size. Likewise, your riser material should be three-quarters of an inch in diameter. Many sprinklers, however, have smaller, half-inch threaded openings on the bottom, and with these you'll need half-inch risers. Your elbows and tees should be ¾ inch S × ¾ inch S × ½ inch T.

### PUTTING IT ALL TOGETHER

Each sprinkler system is different. Once again, your dealer is the best source of information. Still, here are a few tips I've gleaned from experience:

- In each spot where you'll have a sprinkler, you'll need an SST tee (a coupling that lets you make the joint around the corner, and also has a female threaded spot on top for a threaded riser), as well as the riser itself. Look for threaded risers that are slightly flexible, that can be cut to fit—and that'll still have working threads after they're cut off.
- To make an SS (slip-slip) connection, start by dabbing plenty of primer on the end of the male part, then do the same for the inside of the female connection. Next, dab plenty of PVC

glue on the end of the male piece, then swab plenty inside the female. Shove the male part into the female as far as it'll go, then give the male part a quarter turn to set the joint. If you check this a minute or two later, you shouldn't be able to move it at all.

- When connecting two threaded pieces, always wrap some white Teflon tape tightly around the threads of the male part first. This will keep it from leaking.

Good luck, and happy irrigating.

## Aerating Your Lawn

While everyone knows that lawns need water, far fewer people realize that lawns also need plenty of air and nutrients. Heavy soils, especially clay soils, have a tendency over time and wear to get harder and harder, more and more compacted. Eventually there isn't enough air space in the soil to support the growth of a decent lawn.

Lawn aeration also goes by a number of other names, all meaning the same thing. It can be called lawn coring, hole punching, or just punching. Whatever it's called, it's a good idea.

How often should you aerate your lawn? This will depend on the type of grass, the amount of foot traffic it gets, and the type of soil you have. Remember that foot traffic compacts the soil and robs the lawn of needed air in the root zone. Bermuda, fescue, or Saint Augustine lawns in the South should be aerated at least once a year; twice a year would be even better. On heavy clay soils anywhere, it's always a good idea to aerate the lawn once a year. On any kind of soil, lawns that get a good deal of foot traffic will benefit from a yearly aeration as well. Loamy or sandy soils usually need aerating only every other year, unless of course they're getting lots of foot traffic.

If you've never aerated your lawn, it's probably time to do it now. Any areas that get lots of foot traffic and where the grass is thin and hardly growing certainly need aeration. If people have driven their cars over part of your lawn, this, too, will need to be aerated. If you haven't aerated your lawn for several years and it's looking a little shabby, then it's time to aerate it again.

### POWER AERATORS

There are a number of ways to get extra air into the soil. Probably the simplest is to go down to a rental yard and rent a lawn aerator, also sometimes called a coring machine. These are gasoline-powered machines that aren't too much harder to use than a big power lawn mower. Be warned, however, that many of these power aerators are quite heavy; if you're not strong, they might be too much for you to handle. Plan on having someone else give you a hand loading and unloading the aerator from the trailer. Sometimes the best way to use a power aerator is to hire someone experienced to do the job for you.

#### *Potential Pitfall*

Before you hire someone to aerate your lawn, ask him or her for a free estimate of the cost. If it seems high to you, shop around a bit before you hire anyone. It's going to cost you around fifty bucks just for the rental of the aerator if you do it yourself, so if you can get a thousand square feet of lawn aerated by a professional for around a hundred dollars, that's a fair deal.

But if you feel up to a little challenge, go for it! Expect to pay around ten dollars an hour to rent a lawn aerator. Usually they come from the rental yard on a small trailer; you'll need a ball hitch on the back of your car or pickup to pull them. Often, though, you can also rent a temporary ball hitch if needed.

One way to save a little money on the aeration is to talk to your neighbors. One or two of them might well want to get in on this with you. Share the machine, and the cost.

Most power aerators look something like a snowblower. They have a gas motor on the top, wheels on the sides or back, and a big circular wheel in the front with hollow spikes or cylinders on it.

### *Insider's Tip*

Before you get rolling with your power aerator, make sure you clearly mark all the lawn sprinkler heads and any water lines that are close to the surface. It would be a shame to aerate your sprinklers and water lines! An experienced landscaper will usually tag these potential problem spots with small flags. If you hire someone to aerate your lawn for you, ask ahead of time how he or she plans to avoid damaging your sprinkler system.

Lawn aerators can move along at a pretty good clip, and it doesn't take too much longer to aerate an area than it would to mow it. Most typical lawns can be aerated in an hour or less, although most rental places will charge you a two-hour minimum. Before you rent an aerator, get out the yellow pages and take a few minutes to call up several different rental companies. Often there are some very wide differences in prices charged for the exact same machines.

The aerator will dig out little plugs from your lawn that will be a bit thicker than a pencil and several inches long. Few aerators are adjustable for depth, but all you need is a few inches at most—although deeper is better. Most aerators have a power drum with many small, hollow cylinders. The soil will be forced through the cylinders, leaving holes in the lawn. Resist the urge to rake these dirt plugs up after you're done aerating. They do look an awful lot like rat poop all over your yard, but leave them there anyhow. After a couple of weeks of watering, the plugs will dissolve back into the lawn.

There are other devices besides core plugging aerators to use for getting more air into the lawn. One is a very easy-to-use step-on hand aerator. I have one made by Hound Dog Products from Minnesota and it works just fine. The only problem with these tools is that they're slow—real slow if you're planning to do an entire yard. Still, if you just want to do a few small areas of the lawn at a time, these will do the trick, and they are inexpensive and reliable. Step-on hand aerators are also useful for touching up smaller spots here and there. Just put the tool on the ground, step down on it, and two plugs of soil will be pushed up, with two holes for air space left behind. There are also models that have four spikes for four holes at a time. I find that if the soil is at all hard, these are much harder to get down into the ground than two-holers.

There are also any number of other handheld, nonmotorized aerating tools, many which work by driving some kind of spike into the soil. There are even spiked sandals you can strap on over your shoes. Just put these on and walk all over your lawn, making little holes everywhere you go. Actually these work fairly well, though none of the spike-type aerators will be quite as effective as the kinds that actually dig and remove small plugs.

If the soil is bone dry, none of these aerators will work well. There needs to be enough moisture in the soil that the plugging units can get down deep. If you try one of the hand step-on aerators on really dry, hard soil, you'll be lucky to get it to go down half an inch. Soak the lawn first, let it dry out some, and then try the aerator. Even if you're planning to hire out the whole aerating job, I still suggest you give your whole lawn a good, deep soaking several days before the work will be done.

Step-on aerators give you a pretty good workout, and if you're someone like me who enjoys getting a bit of exercise while you work on the lawn, you might enjoy owning one. If, however, you're a type A personality who wants to get things done completely, correctly, and right now, then I suggest you go rent a power aerator.

## SOIL TYPES AND AERATION

If your soil is sandy, you probably only need to go over it once with the power aerator, and it's a good idea to aerate in the same direction that you would normally mow the lawn. If you have heavy clay soil, or loamy soil that's very compacted, then go over the entire lawn with the aerator twice, once from each direction. The plugs that will be all over when you're done can be raked so that most will break up and fall back into the lawn. If you just can't stand the look, rake them up and dump them in your compost heap. Some gardeners will add a layer of river sand over the lawn after they've aerated it. The sand will work its way into the new holes; this supposedly helps with drainage. I'm not totally convinced that adding sand is worth the effort, but if you have access to plenty of free or cheap silty river sand, you might want to give it a try. Do *not* add beach sand—it will be way too salty.

Once you've finished aerating your lawn, this is the perfect time to fertilize and reseed it, too. Chapters 4 and 8 have specific fertilizer and seeding recommendations, but briefly, after the aeration is finished, you'll want to sprinkle on some fertilizer; reseed the entire lawn with grass seed; cover it all with about a quarter of an inch of steer manure, finished compost, river sand, or pulverized peat moss; and irrigate it well. If you know that your soil is acidic, then this is a good time to add some lime. Use dolomite lime and apply about five pounds for every hundred square feet of lawn.

## *Potential Pitfall*

Once you've aerated a lawn, the roots are much more exposed to the air than before, and the entire lawn is now much more open to drying out. Within hours after aerating any lawn, it's important to give it a good soaking. The freshly aerated lawn will remain more susceptible to drying out for several weeks, so be sure it's kept well watered during this entire period.

### AERATING TIPS

- If you have a sod lawn that can't be matched by seed, do not overseed it after aerating. Fertilize it, add some organic matter, keep it well irrigated, and it should come together quickly.

- An exceptionally hot summer day is not the best time to aerate your lawn; you might do too much damage to it. Wait until a cooler day or at least until later in the day. Also, a very hot and windy day will dry out any lawn quickly.
- If the weather is unusually cold, or the days are still not in the sixty-degree-or-warmer stage, then wait awhile until it warms up. A cold lawn can be damaged by aeration.

If you have never before bothered to aerate your lawn, I think you'll be pleasantly surprised with the results. Remember, a lawn needs water and air to grow, and aerating it gets a lot more air into the root zone. Healthy roots almost always equal a healthy, thriving lawn.

CHAPTER 4

# Lawn Fertilizers

## A Word About Soil Tests

You will read over and over that you must do a soil test before applying fertilizer. It's as if someone wants you to feel guilty if you don't. But really, for most of us, testing might not be necessary at all. If your lawn is healthy and growing well, the odds are your pH and fertility levels are just fine.

Still, if you want to have the soil from your own yard tested, it can't hurt. And it's actually easier than you might think: Usually you'll need to send in at least a cup and a half of soil—about a pound—from your yard. Be sure to take soil samples from several different spots, the more the better, and mix them together. Use a clean hand trowel to dig the samples, and don't put them into any container that ever held fertilizer—any residue will yield confused results.

Cornell University offers soil tests where you take a sample, per its online instructions, mail it in with its online form and fifteen dollars, and in a week or so you'll get a printout describing your own soil's strengths and weaknesses. Cornell's soil test link is: http://www.css.cornell.edu/soiltest/soil_testing/index.asp.

Or you can look in the phone book and call up your own state or county Cooperative Extension Office, or your county agriculture office, and ask for information on soil tests. Almost every state offers these tests, which generally cost between five and twenty dollars. The results will show your soil's levels of nitrogen, phosphorus, and potassium, as well as its pH. They will also give specific recommendations on how to bring your own soil up to optimum levels.

In lawns that are irrigated, the levels of nitrogen in particular will change from year to year, so you might want to do a new soil test every couple of years.

You can also buy soil testing kits and do your own soil testing. I wouldn't bother with this, though: The kits are not cheap, and the results may be less than correct. At any rate, you can get a soil test done cheaply, accurately, and quickly through the mail.

### HOW TO PREDICT YOUR OWN SOIL FERTILITY

If you live in a northern area that gets a good deal of rain in summer, odds are that your soil is relatively high in nitrogen, is low in phosphorous and potassium, and has an acidic pH. The flip side of this is that if you live in the Southwest where the summers are hot and dry, you can expect your soil to be quite low in nitrogen, fairly well supplied with phosphorous and potassium, and either alkaline or slightly alkaline in pH. In Southeastern parts of the United States, it's common to find soils that are acidic, low in nitrogen, and moderate in phosphorous and potassium.

This said, many times when a new house is built, all the best topsoil is pushed off somewhere and the lawn is planted on very infertile subsoils. This is one of the reasons that in so many areas we need to constantly keep feeding our lawns. A soil test will take much of the guesswork out of the equation—but please, don't let anyone make you feel guilty if you never bother to take this step.

## NPK

All sacks, boxes, and bottles of fertilizers must by law list clearly what their NPK is. NPK is expressed as numbers, as in 10–12–5. These numbers represent percentages of nitrogen (N), phosphorus (P), and potassium (K). If in the above example the whole sack of fertilizer weighed a hundred pounds, then there would be exactly ten pounds of actual nitrogen, twelve pounds of actual phosphorus, and five pounds of actual potassium.

In this same example, if we were to add up the numbers ten, twelve, and five, we would get a total of twenty-seven pounds of actual fertilizer in this hundred-pound sack. So what's the remaining seventy-three pounds? It's termed "inert ingredients," and it's simply filler.

Pay attention to these NPK numbers on any fertilizer you are considering buying. If a fifty-pound sack of 20–30–20 costs the same as a hundred-pound sack of 8–12–7, then, which is the better buy? It would be the fifty-pound sack, since despite the fact it weighs only half as much and costs the same, it has more actual fertilizer in it. How much more? In this case, there's eight extra pounds of actual (real) fertilizer in the fifty-pound sack.

How does this work? Well, if you combine the NPK numbers in the fifty-pound bag, they total seventy. This number is a percentage, and since this sack is only half as heavy as the other, we have to divide the seventy by two. This gives us thirty-five pounds of actual fertilizer. The larger hundred-pound sack's NPK numbers add up to twenty-seven. This is (conveniently!) a hundred-pound sack, and 100 percent equals twenty-seven.

The point is this: Don't be fooled by the size of the sack, box, or jug of fertilizer. Look at the NPK numbers and see for yourself how much is fertilizer and how much is filler. The filler is generally next to worthless.

## *Insider's Tip*

Buy your fertilizer at a farm supply store. You don't have to be a farmer to shop at these places. I like to buy lawn fertilizer in fifty-, eighty-, or hundred-pound sacks. Often the price you pay for an eighty-pound sack of fertilizer at a farm supply store will actually be less than what you might pay for a twenty-pound sack at a different store.

## Nitrogen (N)

Each element in a sack of fertilizer has a somewhat different purpose. Nitrogen is almost always the most important fertilizer element for plant growth, and especially so for grass lawns. Adequate nitrogen brings out the deeper green colors of lawns. A lawn low in nitrogen will be lighter green in color.

Nitrogen is necessary for the growth of stems and leaves. A lawn low in available nitrogen will grow slowly and won't be as thick. When a lawn grows too slowly, it doesn't smother out competing weeds. Lawns low in nitrogen quickly become weedy. Nitrogen encourages the growth of grasses at the expense of competing broadleaf weeds such as clovers or dandelions. Adequate nitrogen is also necessary for overall plant health, and lack of nitrogen can lead to increased susceptibility to attack by insects and disease.

Areas with low summer rainfall often have soils that are very low in nitrogen. To establish and maintain a decent lawn in these areas, fertilizers with enough supplemental nitrogen must be used.

Areas with high summer rainfall, especially in the Midwest, often have soils already supplied with considerable nitrogen. In these areas, less nitrogen fertilizer will be needed each year.

Unlike phosphorus or potassium, nitrogen can travel fast through the soil and quickly be leached out from heavy rain or overwatering. Because nitrogen leaches quickly, if you want a choice-looking lawn, this is one fertilizer ingredient you may need to reapply numerous times during each year.

Nitrogen leaches downward fastest in sandy soils, and slowest in heavy clay soils. Because of this, if your own soil is sandy, you'll need to fertilize your lawns more frequently in order to keep them at their best.

Most lawns will need between two and eight pounds of actual nitrogen per thousand square feet, per year. To get square feet, multiply the length of the lawn times the width. Thus, a lawn twenty feet wide and fifty feet long is a thousand square feet. Buffalo grass lawns need as little as two pounds of actual nitrogen per thousand square feet, while fast-growing lawns such as Saint Augustine can easily use six to eight pounds per year. Lawns on sandy soils will need more nitrogen per year than those growing on loam or clay soils. For details on how much nitrogen each species of grass needs, see the chart in appendix B.

It is always best to split applications of nitrogen fertilizer. For example, assume you had a thousand-square-foot Saint Augustine lawn that you intended to give eight pounds of actual N per year. If you were using ammonium sulfate (21–0–0), to get one pound of actual N you'd need about five pounds of fertilizer. Thus, for this lawn you would use a max of eight times five, or forty pounds of ammonium sulfate. You'd be wise to split this into two applications of twenty pounds each, rather than putting on all forty pounds at once.

Outside temperature affects the speed at which nitrogen is taken up and used by plants. The warmer the weather, the quicker will be the uptake of nitrogen. Ammonium forms of nitrogen must first convert to nitrate forms before the grasses can actually make use of the N. In warm weather, this happens quickly, but in cold weather it's slow. Nitrate forms of fertilizer are very fast acting and will go to work immediately.

### *Insider's Tip*

No matter what kind of fertilizer you use, whenever you fertilize a lawn it's important to give it a good soaking immediately afterward. Never put on any lawn fertilizer and then just lightly sprinkle the lawn. Think of this as insurance against possible fertilizer burn.

## TOO MUCH NITROGEN

Too much nitrogen quickly causes problems. Excessive nitrogen will also cause long, weak stems, resulting in grass that lies flat. Too much nitrogen can also stimulate the growth of fungal molds. And it will burn a lawn and result in dead grass. This burning of the grass will usually occur within twenty-four hours of the overapplication, so you'll know right away!

If you ever suddenly discover that you put on too much nitrogen fertilizer, immediately start soaking the lawn! If you add enough water to it, you'll leach the nitrogen down past the root zone, and your lawn will be okay.

Many years ago, a coworker of mine spread ammonium sulfate fertilizer on the front lawn of a home we were landscaping. Ammonium sulfate has an NPK reading of 21–0–0; it's 21 percent actual nitrogen. The lawn was about twenty feet wide by thirty feet long, or six hundred square feet. It was a Bermuda grass lawn, a little on the yellow side and not showing too much growth each week. Now, we would usually apply about four pounds of actual nitrogen to a thousand square feet of Bermuda grass lawn. This would mean about twenty pounds of ammonium sulfate for a thousand square feet, and thus about twelve pounds for a lawn of this size, six hundred square feet.

I asked my friend how much fertilizer he'd put on and he said, "The whole bag, of course."

It was a hundred-pound sack of ammonium sulfate! I did some quick figuring in my head and realized he'd put on almost ten times more than he should have. If we lightly sprinkled that lawn, it would be dead in a matter of hours. What I did was turn on the sprinklers full blast and let them run for the entire day. When it got dark, I turned them off for about an hour to let it soak in, and then I turned them back on again. I knew if I didn't get most of that nitrogen to leach down past the root zone, we'd be in deep trouble. I soaked the lawn until about nine o'clock that evening, then shut it down and went home.

The next morning the lawn still looked okay, so I turned on the sprinklers again and soaked it for hours more.

A week later that lawn was the deepest green you'd ever seen—and half a foot high besides. We mowed it, bagging the profuse clippings, and when we were done we'd filled three huge trash cans. The lawn grew like that for several weeks before it settled down, but we didn't kill any of the grass.

There are many different types of nitrogen fertilizer. Ammonium sulfate is cheap, fast acting, and has 21 percent nitrogen as well as containing some sulfur. Since sulfur is acidic, this is a good fertilizer to use on soil that's naturally on the alkaline side. In areas with heavy summer rainfall, soil is often acidic. Where summer rainfall is light, it's usually alkaline. When you fertilize a lawn growing on an acidic soil, it's often best to use something that won't add to the acidity. Sodium nitrate, with an NPK usually of 16–0–0, is less acidic than ammonium sulfate and thus a better choice for acidic soils. Manures—which I'll discuss further in chapter 11, on organic methods—are generally somewhat alkaline and work well on acidic soils.

Urea is a fertilizer that some believe is made from urine, but actually isn't. Urea is classified as a "synthetic organic" fertilizer. You could say that while urea is technically organic, it is by no means "natural." At any rate, it can be bought in several strengths, most commonly as either 42–0–0 or 48–0–0. Because of its organic makeup, urea is slower acting than most other granular chemical fertilizers. This slow-release action can be very beneficial for lawns, releasing nitrogen over an extended period of time.

## *Insider's Tip*

Earthworms and other smaller soil microorganisms are good for the health of the soil, and for the health of the lawn. Earthworms aerate the soil and add humus. There are those who claim that all chemical fertilizer kills off these beneficial soil creatures, but I haven't seen this happen when fertilizer was used judiciously. There is no doubt that overheavy application of fertilizer, especially high-nitrogen kinds, will kill many microorganisms and earthworms. The main point is: Use the recommended amount of fertilizer and no more.

## Phosphorus (P)

Phosphorus is necessary for the growth of plants, especially for root and flower growth. With lawns, you don't care about flowering—in fact, you'd rather the grass didn't flower. But strong, healthy, vigorous roots have everything to do with having a terrific lawn.

Because phosphorus doesn't travel well in the soil, it's slow to leach out. Applying phosphate fertilizers once a year is usually all you need to do. The exceptions might be in areas with very long growing seasons and high summer rainfall, such as in Florida or parts of southeastern Texas, where two applications of fertilizer with phosphorus are often needed. There is sometimes another exception: areas where there are very low amounts of phosphorus already in the soil and where the lawns are being micromanaged to be at their optimum all season long.

Phosphorus levels will be lowest where summer rainfall is highest. In other words, in areas where nitrogen is naturally abundant, phosphorus usually isn't.

If you are growing ground covers that flower or flowering trees or shrubs, these will need more phosphorus than will your lawn. In the drier, Western areas of the United States, phosphorus levels are usually decent; applying too much phosphorus would just encourage weeds to grow and flower in your lawn.

Phosphorus can be purchased in mixes or as a single-element fertilizer. "Superphosphate" usually has an NPK of 0–18–0, and triple superphosphate or treble phosphate has a reading of 0–45–0. In low-phosphorus areas, a lawn can usually be improved by applying several pounds of P each year. This would amount to slightly more than four pounds of 0–45–0.

## Potassium (K)

Like phosphorus, potassium levels are generally low where nitrogen is abundant and are high where summers are warm and dry. Adequate potassium is necessary for all plant life; it helps build strong stems and makes plants more disease resistant, healthier, and better able to withstand cold winter conditions. Potassium also helps lawns repair faster from stress from too much foot traffic, drought, or high summer heat. Unlike nitrogen, potassium doesn't leach out of the soil quickly, and so it doesn't need to be applied frequently. In cold-winter areas, many wise gardeners like to apply potassium in late summer or early fall. These late applications ensure that the grass will make it through the long dormant period. Late potassium fertilizers are recommended for any warm-season grass that will be dormant for several months or longer.

Potassium can be bought as part of a fertilizer mix, or you can get an all-potassium fertilizer. The most common potassium fertilizers are potassium sulfate (0–0–50) and potassium chloride (0–0–60). Either can burn plants if applied too heavily, especially the potassium chloride. To avoid fertilizer burning: Apply only the recommended amount, apply fertilizer later in the day when the temperatures have cooled down, and do not apply granular fertilizer to wet grass. Once you've applied any lawn fertilizers, always follow with a thorough irrigation, never a light sprinkling.

Applications of potassium don't seem to encourage weed growth as much as excessive phosphorus does. Gardeners will find that high potassium levels in their vegetable gardens results in sweeter cucumbers and lettuce, and roses that produce more flowers and longer, stronger stems.

Because neither potassium nor phosphorus travels well in the soil, it's always a good idea to work these two elements into the soil before planting any new lawn (or shrub, or tree, or ground cover).

## Luxury Consumption

If you apply too much phosphorus (P) or potassium (K), the result is usually not burning of the plants. Rather, the typical result of using more phosphorus or potassium than is actually needed is called luxury consumption. What this means is that the plants (the grasses) will use as much of these elements as they need, and then will also take up and use more than needed—hence the name. This extra consumption doesn't harm the grass itself, but it adds nothing and is a waste of money.

Too much phosphorus will encourage weeds to grow, especially nongrass weeds such as clover, dandelion, cheeseweed, and plantain. If you live in the dry-summer areas of the country, such as the Southwest, the soil often has plenty of phosphorus and potassium. Adding more of these elements just encourages luxury consumption and, even worse, more weeds in your lawn. In California where I live, I have always been able to maintain good lawns without using "complete" fertilizers. Once in a blue moon I might apply some fertilizer with phosphorus and potassium, but even then I don't think it's necessary. Here, what we need is extra nitrogen.

### *Potential Pitfall*

Even though many books, experts, and nursery personnel insist that you need to use a "complete" fertilizer (one with N, P, and K), they might not always be right.

## Weed-and-Feed Fertilizers

There will be more on this subject in the next chapter, on weeds and herbicides, but one point here: For some reason most of the so-called complete fertilizers you can buy contain lawn herbicides. In many areas, using these weed-and-feed blends will add more phosphorus (P) than is needed. The herbicide in the fertilizer will kill off most of the existing broadleaf weeds (dandelions, clovers, and so forth) in the lawn, but the extra, unneeded phosphorus will encourage more weeds to grow once the herbicide breaks down. This makes me wonder:

Seems like as long as you use the stuff now and then, you'll keep having weeds in your lawn. Sure, if you use it every six weeks you'll get rid of the weeds, but still. Doesn't it seem as if the fertilizer companies are almost making sure you'll need to keep using it over and over?

## Micronutrients

Micronutrients such as iron, manganese, zinc, and boron may occasionally be needed to keep a lawn looking its best. There are some complete lawn fertilizers that have NPK and micronutrients. These fertilizers cost more, but if they're what you need, then they're worth it. Soil pH (see below) may also impact on needs for micronutrients. But to really tell for sure, you would need a good soil test. Most of us are able to grow very decent lawns without ever worrying about micronutrients. One way to ensure that your lawn gets micronutrients is to apply a thin layer of steer manure each year.

## Some Things You *Don't* Need

You'll see plenty of ads in which people swear up and down that liquid fertilizers are the best way to a fabulous lawn. Don't believe them. These are usually applied with a jar sprayer attached directly to the end of a garden hose. These water-soluble fertilizers are often fast acting and fairly effective, but they are not at all cost effective. My advice: Don't waste your money on these. They may be helpful on flowers or ground covers, but they just won't get enough actual fertilizer onto a lawn to do much good. At any rate, on a pound-per-pound basis, compared to most other lawn fertilizers, liquid fertilizers are extremely expensive.

This also applies to all those other water-soluble fertilizers that come in granular form, often in plastic bags packed in small boxes. These are versions of fertilizer you'd normally use on houseplants. And for houseplants, they're terrific. But for lawns, forget it! Not effective enough and too expensive.

Fertilizers that are coated and release over an extended period of time, such as Osmocote, are wonderful for potted plants, but for lawns they are far too expensive and not needed in the least. If you want time-release fertilizer for a lawn, I suggest using urea or some organic fertilizer, such as steer manure.

## pH

Soil acidity or alkalinity is described as soil pH. The pH scale runs from 1 through 14. A pH of 1 is totally acidic, such as sulfuric acid. A pH of 14 is purely alkaline—lye, for instance. The middle of the pH scale is the number 7, which is considered neutral. At a pH of 7, most plants and lawns will grow just fine. Soils below 7 are considered acidic, and soils over 7 are alkaline.

There are exceptions, though; many plants, including azaleas, camellias, rhododendrons, and blueberries, will only grow well on acidic soils. And a few plants such as lilacs and cantaloupes grow best on slightly alkaline soil.

If a soil is too acidic (below 6) or too alkaline (above 7.5), the uptake of macro- and micronutrients is often negatively affected. This is most commonly seen on Western soils where the pH may be excessively alkaline and the uptake of iron (Fe) is poor. Often there will be plenty of iron in the soil even though the lawn and other landscape plants are all showing symptoms of lack of iron. You can run a magnet through this soil and it will quickly be covered with iron, yet the plants are starved for it. What you will generally see with iron-deficient plants are leaves that are light green with leaf veins that are dark green. This condition is called iron chlorosis, and affected plants are said to be chlorotic.

If your lawn is chlorotic, you can apply fertilizer with added iron, but the more sensible thing to do would be to try to lower the soil pH itself. Aluminum sulfate can be used to lower pH, but it's fairly expensive. Fertilizers such as ammonium sulfate have sulfur in them and their use will lower pH somewhat.

## SOIL SULFUR

An ideal pH for lawns is somewhere between 6.5 and 7.4. Where soils are highly alkaline—with pH readings of 7.7 and higher—soil sulfur might be worth using as a preplanting material. It will lower soil pH. Most people, though, won't need to bother with soil sulfur. Do not apply too much of this material to an existing lawn—it can burn leaves. It's also stinky when wet, so if you do use soil sulfur, only apply it on a dry lawn. Do not apply soil sulfur on days where the temperature is above eighty-five degrees, because burning could be the result. See the chart in appendix B on how much soil sulfur to use to lower pH.

## LIME

Think of lime as the opposite of soil sulfur. Lime has a high pH, so you'd only add it to a soil that was quite acidic, to raise the pH. A soil that tests below 6.5 is probably too acidic to grow optimum grass, and would benefit from some additional lime. See the chart in appendix B for exact amounts.

Lime can burn a lawn, too, and most of us can have perfectly good lawns without ever applying it. But if you live in the East or Southeast, in any areas with high summer rainfall, you might indeed have soil that's quite acidic and could use some lime. The best lime is calcium carbonate.

## GYPSUM

Gypsum, which comes in sacks as a white powdery material, is calcium sulfate. As such, it's a mix of material that is both alkaline and acidic, and is itself neutral in pH. Gypsum adds both calcium and sulfur to the soil, and both are important for plant growth. The main use for gypsum is in the manufacture of plaster products, including stucco, wall and ceiling boards, moldings, as well as sculpturing plasters, medical and dental uses, and pottery. Gypsum is very inexpensive, and if you buy it at a brickyard where plasterers shop, the price is much lower than at a nursery. Construction gypsum works just fine in the yard; material labeled "horticultural gypsum" is no better at all.

Gypsum has terrific effects on soil structure and will make heavy clay soils looser. Adding gypsum to soils improves soil drainage, adds nutrients, and improves structure. You can sprinkle gypsum over the top of a lawn and then water it in. For most lawns, use about ten pounds of gypsum per thousand square feet. This can be repeated several times each year with good effects. The gypsum will also act to smother a large number of lawn insect pests. Just be sure to soak it in after applying it.

Adding gypsum before you seed or sod a lawn is almost always a good idea. It's pretty much impossible to add too much gypsum, but for soil preparation for new lawns, add fifty pounds per thousand square feet of soil. In dry-summer, Western areas, this can be increased to a hundred pounds of gypsum per thousand square feet. Gypsum is also good for soils that tend to get salty; it makes it much easier for the harmful salts to leach down far below the root zone of the lawn.

By the way, if you have a small pond, adding some gypsum to the water tends to reduce algal growth and makes the water clearer.

## Applying Fertilizer: Fertilizer Spreaders

I have a small hopper-top, whirlybird-type fertilizer spreader that is easy to use. The main problem with this spreader is that if there is any moisture at all in the fertilizer, the clumps will stop it up. I then have to dump it, break up or remove all the clumps, and start all over. I like to use ammonium sulfate, ammonium nitrate, and calcium nitrate fertilizers, and all of these will quickly get clumpy if allowed to soak up any moisture. Keep your fertilizer dry! You can usually buy one of these one-handed spreaders for less than twelve bucks.

More effective are the larger whirlybird-type spreaders on wheels, with larger open hopper tops. You just pour the fertilizer in the hopper, set the spreader to the rate you want, and then walk around the yard as the fertilizer is whirled out. I've seen these on sale in spring for less than seventeen dollars.

The old-fashioned but perfectly effective drop-type spreaders also have large open hopper tops. Fill the top with granular lawn fertilizer, set the application rate, and start spreading. Although these probably do a better job than any of the other spreaders, the main question is, To overlap or not to overlap? If you put on fertilizer at a heavy rate and overlap too much, you'll get burn lines. If you fertilize at a heavy rate and don't overlap at all, you may easily get yellow grass lines where the lawn didn't get any fertilizer. I see these drop spreaders often on sale for less than twenty bucks.

Any of the above spreaders is good, and you should own one of them. If you're new to using these, just put in a small amount of fertilizer and spread it at a low application rate. See how it works and get it all figured out before you get down to serious fertilization of your lawn.

The bottom line is that a high-quality lawn will need some kind of fertilizer.

CHAPTER 5

# Herbicides and Weeds

## Weeds

The common definition of *weed* is, "any plant growing out of place." Thus, a plum tree sprouting in a cornfield is a weed, as is a geranium growing in your tomato patch. But with lawns, there really are only two groups of weeds: grasses and broadleaf weeds.

How might a grass be a weed in a lawn? Well, if you have a nice Bermuda grass lawn and crabgrass starts to sprout in it, it's a weed all right. Likewise, if you have a great fescue lawn and Bermuda grass sprouts, that Bermuda grass is now a weed. Again, a weed is a plant growing where you don't want it to grow.

Broadleaf weeds, such as dandelions, clovers, and plantains, are not grasses, but in lawns they're almost always considered weeds. An herbicide that will kill one kind of broadleaf weed will almost always kill every other kind of broadleaf weed as well. There is little reason that you need to be able to identify every species of weed that pops up in your lawn.

Your number one defense against weeds is to keep your lawn growing vigorously. Lawns that are kept regularly mowed, well fertilized, well watered, and aerated and overseeded yearly have few weeds. A healthy, vigorous lawn can be kept pretty much weed-free simply by checking it every few weeks and then digging up any new weeds you see by hand. Get out that pocketknife and put it to work!

If your lawn is already quite weedy, the weeds first need to be brought under control. This can be done by hand or with herbicides, or with a little bit of both.

### WEED DIGGERS

There are a lot of different weed diggers on the market, and most of them work pretty well. If you don't mind bending over while you work, the old-fashioned long-shanked dandelion diggers work just great. The dandelion may well grow back from the part of the root left in the ground. You may find that you dig the same dandelion five or six times before you actually kill it. Think of it as exercise. All that bending over is good for the waistline.

I have found that an old pocketknife works pretty well as a dandelion digger. If I spot a big dandelion in my lawn and the digger isn't handy, I just take out my pocketknife and dig out the weed. Of course, the dirt soon dulls any sharpness the blade may have. Many of the head groundskeepers of professional baseball teams do not use herbicides on their highly manicured lawns. For example, at the famous Wrigley Field, home of the Chicago Cubs, they never use herbicides. They remove any weeds by hand.

For a lawn that is pretty much out of control with the weeds, you can try the following before you resort to herbicides: Fertilize heavily, using two pounds of ammonium sulfate per hundred square feet of lawn. Add a layer of steer manure, too, about a quarter inch deep, and keep it all well watered for a few weeks. Sometimes you can get the grass to just outgrow most of the weeds. Once the grass is growing fast, then get to work with the dandelion digger.

Still, if your lawn is really weedy with broadleaf weeds, getting it under control may well mean resorting to an herbicide. Think of this as a onetime use, not as something you'll be doing over and over. Once you have the weeds pretty well killed off, then you need to get the grass growing strongly and keep it growing well, so it will outcompete the weeds.

## Herbicides (Weed Killers)

There are a number of different herbicides (*herb* means "plant," and *cide* means "killer") you can use on your lawn. Most common are "selective" broadleaf weed killers, which selectively kill off weeds such as dandelions, clovers, purslane, spurge, and other broadleaf weeds, but do not kill grasses. Most of these contain a chemical called 2,4-D, and while it is effective, there are some major concerns connected to its use. Actually, there are major concerns with the use of any type of herbicide.

I used to own a retail nursery, and every spring and summer I would see customer after customer—always men—urgently wanting to buy large, potted arborvitae shrubs. These are expensive plants, and I was always more than happy to make the sale. But when I asked them why they needed them, the answer was almost always the same.

These guys had decided to spray their lawns with dandelion killer and had done so on windy days. The weed killer had drifted over to a neighbor's yard and had promptly killed the neighbor's prized arborvitae bushes. It usually only took a few days for the damage to be apparent, and suddenly they were in need of big replacement bushes.

Likewise, when I was teaching horticulture at a school where we had a large rose garden, I once made the mistake of letting a careless student spray Roundup (a nonselective herbicide) on weeds growing near the roses. By the end of the day, the roses were beginning to wilt and die. As I remember, the roses died off faster than the weeds did!

## SOME NOTES ON SPRAYING HERBICIDES

Pump sprayers are the most common devices for spraying herbicides. I've used a great many pump sprayers over the years, and my main advice is: Buy several of them, and buy the cheap ones! Metal sprayers are far more expensive than the heavy plastic kind, and after time they will rust and start plugging up repeatedly. Get the plastic. I like to have two sprayers, a small one gallon one for spraying herbicide and another two-gallon model for spraying insecticides. Take an indelible black felt marker and clearly write on one sprayer, INSECTICIDE ONLY! On the other one print, boldly and clearly, HERBICIDE ONLY!

- Never use the herbicide sprayer for spraying any fungicides or insecticides. If you need to spray with a fungicide, use the sprayer you have marked for insecticides.
- When you are using a pump sprayer, keep a small piece of wire in your pocket. If the tip gets plugged up, clear it with the wire.
- If and when you do decide to spray an herbicide of any kind, first check whether it's at all windy or breezy out. If so, don't do it!
- If you're spraying herbicide, keep the spray tip very close to the weeds themselves—just inches away. It's way too easy to drift some of the herbicide onto your ornamental plants.
- On very hot, dry days, spray-on herbicides are exceptionally effective, and if there is any drift at all, it will do plenty of unintended damage.
- Also note that on hot, dry days, if you exceed the recommended amount of the herbicide on your lawn, you'll kill off large amounts of lawn. Even selective herbicides applied too heavily will kill a lawn.
- Some lawn herbicides are applied in granular form, and overapplication of these will also quickly kill off even the healthiest lawn.
- Saint Augustine grasses are not tolerant of 2,4-D type herbicides. Instead, you need an herbicide specifically made for Saint Augustine grass.

## FERTILIZERS WITH HERBICIDE

The so-called feed-and-weed or weed-and-feed fertilizers are handy, but far too many of them come with "complete" fertilizers that have large amounts of phosphorus. In many lawns, especially Western lawns, additional phosphorus will usually just encourage more broadleaf weeds to grow. Nitrogen encourages grasses to grow, and additional phosphorus encourages clover to grow. My first advice on these fertilizer–weed killer combinations is to buy only those high in nitrogen (N) and low in phosphorus (P). See chapter 4 to better understand this.

## HEALTH ISSUES

Numerous studies have shown serious health problems associated with the use of lawn herbicides and lawn insecticides. Some of the data suggest a possible link between incidence of leukemia and herbicide use. With this in mind, do you have young children who will be playing on your lawn? If so, I suggest you go sparingly (if at all) with these lawn herbicides. Rather than applying granular fertilizer with herbicide in it to your entire lawn, it would be far safer for the kids if you spot-sprayed individual weeds in the lawn with a liquid mix. But even with this, be sure not to let the children play on a treated lawn for at least a week, and make darn sure you don't track any of this herbicide into the house on the soles of your shoes.

Anytime you're spraying any kind of herbicide or pesticide, start at the far end of the lawn and work backward. Do *not* walk on the area you have just sprayed.

## LAWN CARE COMPANIES

I won't name names here, but it was well publicized recently that among clients of a large lawn care company that routinely sprays lawns with a chemical fertilizer, herbicide, fungicide, and insecticide mix, women had a greater-than-average chance of getting breast cancer. These lawns looked darn good, they were green and thick and there were very few weeds in them, but hey, breast cancer? For my money, it isn't worth the risks involved.

If you insist on a close-to-perfect lawn, you'd be safer to do the spraying yourself, and never spray any more than is necessary.

I like a nice lawn as much as the next guy, probably more, but I like my wife way more than any lawn. At any rate, always take great care with any lawn fungicides (fungus killers), herbicides, and pesticides (insect killers).

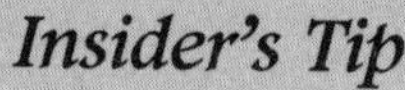


Golf courses are treated with more insecticides, fungicides, and herbicides than any other lawns. This chemical residue will stick to your golf tees, your shoes, and more. Never stick a golf tee in your mouth, and change your golf shoes before you get home. Don't track the chemicals into your house.

### HOW ABOUT OUR PETS?

One last note here on health problems associated with use, and especially overuse, of lawn chemicals. How about our pets?

Dogs and cats spend a lot of time rolling around in the grass, and any chemical we apply to the lawn could affect them. Pets like to eat grass, and grass that has been treated cannot be good for them. Off the subject here, but worth noting again nonetheless, is that for many animals fescue grass can be poisonous. If you have a dog that loves to eat grass, fescue probably isn't the wisest choice for a lawn.

Cats, because they lick themselves so often, are especially vulnerable to chemically treated lawns. Lawn chemicals have also been shown to increase the frequency and severity of allergies for dogs and cats—and for the pets' owners.

Although broadleaf weed killers for lawns are still widely used and sold in almost all nurseries, there are some interesting concerns with these products and the health of our pets, dogs in particular. Almost all these so-called dandelion killers use the chemical 2,4-D. Back in September 1991, a study published in the *Journal of the National Cancer Institute* said that when people used a 2,4-D herbicide on their lawns four or more times a year, dogs that played on those lawns were twice as likely to develop a cancer called malignant lymphoma. On lawns where this herbicide was used only once each year, the dogs still had a cancer risk that was one-third higher than that of dogs on nonherbicided lawns.

It is worth noting here, too, that workers who mixed and sprayed 2,4-D more than twenty days per year were up to three times more likely to develop lymphatic cancer. Lymphatic cancer has increased in Americans by about 50 percent since 1973. It's something worth thinking about.

So does all this mean we should never use any lawn chemicals? No, I don't think so. I think it means we should use them sparingly. We should use organic methods where they work. And we should always consider learning to enjoy a lawn that looks really nice, but that might not be totally "perfect."

Beauty *is* in the eye of the beholder. If your lawn pleases you and looks great to you, then that's a beautiful lawn.

CHAPTER 6

# Lawn Mowers and Goats

"The Perfect Lawn Mower. Get a Goat!"

I read the above advice recently in an article that advised you could "throw away your lawn mower and buy a goat" instead. The goat would even trim your shrubs and hedges, it said. A goat doesn't need any gasoline, doesn't need its oil checked, has no blades that needed sharpening, and makes a terrific pet.

Sound like good advice?

Well, think again. Replacing your lawn mower with a goat might well be some of the very worst gardening advice I have *ever* seen in print! Years ago when I owned a farm, someone gave me three goats. Seemed like a pretty good deal to me at the time. The price was right and what the heck; the goats could mow my lawn for me. Right?

Wrong!

I quickly learned that goats don't like to be tethered. They almost instantly wrap themselves up in the rope and are soon bleating bloody murder as they continue to try to choke themselves to death. The second thing I found out was that fences don't impress goats very much. They can climb fences (and darn near anything else, too, including your car, your shed, and your house) and are experts at getting loose.

When a goat gets loose, it does what goats like to do most. Eat your grass, right? Mow the lawn?

No!

Goats like to eat all right, but they don't give a fig for eating grass, not when they can mow down your cherry trees, apple trees, plum trees, or rosebushes. Given half a chance, a goat or two (or—shudder—three of 'em) will destroy any nice landscape you have, and in quick order, too.

I guess in all fairness to goats, I ought to mention that they actually do like to eat poison ivy and poison oak, so if you want to clear some land, okay, get the goats. But as far as replacing your lawn mower with them . . . take the expert advice here: Don't do it! Even if they're free.

## Nonmotorized Reel-type Push Lawn Mowers

We might as well start with the most basic of all lawn mowers, the hand-push kind. These have some very real advantages:

- They need no gasoline or electricity.
- They always start.
- They are safer than other lawn mowers.
- They don't pollute the air.
- They do less damage to a lawn than most power mowers.
- They make very little noise.
- They provide the owner with good exercise.
- Newer models are lightweight and can often be picked up and carried with one hand.
- They leave the grass clippings well distributed behind the mower; raking up these clippings is rarely necessary, or even desirable. Clippings, when evenly distributed, provide the lawn with slow-release fertilizer and are quite beneficial.
- They are dependable.

I suggest everyone have one of these mowers as a backup unit. When everything else fails, you can get this one out and mow your lawn. But these mowers have their drawbacks, too:

- They do a poor job of cutting weeds, such as tall dandelion heads.
- Many of them will not mow a lawn as low as you might like.
- While they cut fine-bladed grasses fairly well, they do a poor job of cutting broader-bladed grasses. They're considerably less effective on lawns with mixed species of grass present.
- You may well have to go over sections of the lawn several times in order to have it all decently mowed.

I recently tried out a new Great States push mower. Unfortunately, it didn't cut grass quite as well as I would have liked, but it did have some new features that older push mowers usually lack. The mowing height was very quick and easy to adjust. The mower is strong but lightweight: The average gardener ought to be able to easily pick it up and carry it with one hand. I'd gladly recommend a Great States mower as a backup. It's made here in the United States, is easy to push, and has a solid feel to it. I have used this mower on a bluegrass lawn, and it did a fine job of cutting. I expect it would work fine with bent grass or any fine-bladed lawn grass. With the broader-bladed grasses, it is less than perfect. That said, however, I find that I'm using this lawn mower more and more often, simply because it's so easy—and kind of fun, too.

## Rotary Mowers

A rotary mower is the basic power lawn mower. It's the least expensive to buy, the easiest to locate, and the easiest to maintain. While it's still true that you often get what you pay for, with rotary lawn mowers you can still get a good deal for a low price.

The first thing to consider when buying a rotary mower is how big the engine is. How much horsepower does it have? More is better here. Don't even consider buying a rotary lawn mower with less than three and a half horsepower. It will be too weak and underpowered, and the engine probably won't last long.

A four- or five-horsepower mower will probably be powerful enough for most average lawns. The larger the engine, the heavier the mower will be. For smaller people, a somewhat smaller mower might be a good idea, easier to use. Check the weight of a lawn mower before you buy a new one. Consider this, too: What you'd like is a mower that has enough power but isn't too heavy.

If you have a lawn that's thick, tough, and normally fairly hard to mow, do consider a power mower with the larger engine. If your lawn is quite large, by all means buy one with a larger engine. A mower with a three- to four-horsepower motor may last a long time if it's only used once a week to mow a small yard or two. But for big lawns, get a powerful motor. With all small gas-powered equipment, the larger engines tend to last longer. This is as true with chain saws and weed whips as it is with lawn mowers. The same thing can be said for electric mowers: The higher-horsepower motors usually have longer lives.

Quite a few lawn mower companies are now selling six-and-a-half-horsepower mowers, and for large lawns these might make plenty of sense. If you're shopping for a new power mower, you'll also see that some of the Japanese auto companies are now building and selling mowers with overhead valve (OHV) engines. These are superior engines and are sometimes worth the extra money it costs to buy one. I have noticed, by the way, that OHV mowers can sometimes be had over the Internet for considerably less than the normal retail price.

## MOWER CUTTING WIDTH

At first you might assume that the wider the mower cuts, the better, but that's not necessarily true at all. If you buy a three-and-a-half-horsepower mower that has more than an eighteen-inch cutting width, then the machine will be underpowered in thick grass. For a twenty-inch mower, you'll want at least four horsepower. If you're looking to buy a mower that will last a long time, consider buying a high-horsepower unit with a twenty-one-inch or smaller mowing width.

## PUSH OR SELF-PROPELLED?

You can buy a power mower that you push yourself, or you can get one that moves itself along, self-propelled. Which is better? For starters, you'll often pay several hundred dollars more for the same mower in a self-propelled version. The self-propelled mowers are easy to use, take little effort to operate, and are handy if you're mowing sloping lawns where it is difficult to push a mower uphill.

Still, if you're in reasonably good shape and your lawn isn't overly huge or steep, the power push mower might be the better choice. It takes power to move the mower along, and any power used to do this job is taken from the mower's ability to cut thick grass. If you do buy a self-propelled lawn mower, consider getting one with the largest engine offered.

Consider, too, that with a self-propelled mower, any extra work an engine does will cause it to burn more gas and to have a somewhat shorter engine life expectancy. It's just one more thing that can break with age.

Lastly, consider the exercise factor. If you mow your lawn once a week, you can count on burning up quite a few calories and getting some needed exercise. If you push your own lawn mower, you'll be getting double the exercise and burn more calories. Over the course of a year, this could add up to a few unwanted pounds you might not gain. As you can probably tell, I like using a push mower myself.

## LAWN MOWER WHEELS

Wheels on power mowers range from high-quality ball-bearing-loaded models to the cheap, stamped-from-thin-metal, no-bearing kind. Cheap wheels make any mower harder to push, and they will often wear out long before the rest of the mower does.

The best lawn mower wheels are large and have ball bearings. As with fishing reels, or with most things that go round and round, the more ball bearings, the better. And wider is better than thinner. A wider wheel won't cut into the lawn as much and won't leave wheel marks as you mow.

## WHEEL ADJUSTMENT

Also pay attention to how easy or difficult it is to adjust these wheels. Generally, the mowing height of a lawn mower is adjusted by lowering or raising the wheels. Many mowers claim to have eight or nine position height adjusters. This is all good, but the main question is, How easy are they to adjust? I like wheel admustment to be easy, simple, and fast. On some mowers, you actually have to get out a wrench, remove the wheel, and then raise or lower its position. You need to do all four wheels, of course, which is both annoying and time consuming. Don't waste your money on a lawn mower like this. Before you ever buy a new one, try adjusting the wheels. See for yourself how easy it is.

## SIDE-BAGGERS OR REAR-BAGGERS?

A side-discharge rotary mower can be used without a bag or catcher, and this might be useful if you're trying to mow down some ivy or some other tall ground cover. A side-discharge mower without a catcher will also pick up and throw (hard, too) small rocks or pieces of wood or metal—something to keep in mind when using one.

A rear-bagging mower can never be used without the catcher attached, because it will shower you with clippings.

If a side-bagging mower and a rear-bagging mower cost the same, you'd be better off with the rear-bagger. Before you buy any new mower, remove the catcher and see if it's easy to replace. Pretend that it's loaded with heavy grass clippings and see if you can figure out how simple it is (or isn't) to empty. I've seen plenty of power mowers that are a royal pain in the rear to empty and then hook back on. What you want, again, is a system that's simple, quick, and easy.

## MULCHING OR NONMULCHING?

For most lawns, mulching mowers are best. The clippings are pulverized and deposited under the mower. They will decompose and add nitrogen back to the lawn. With fescue lawns, though, the clippings don't break down very well and often just add up as thatch. Still, for almost all lawns except fescue, a mulching mower is a good idea. Some lawn mowers now have a feature that enables you to either mulch or use the machine as a side-bagger that catches the clippings as you go.

## PRICE, QUALITY, AND NAME BRANDS

Unfortunately, there are a number of lawn mowers on the market these days that just aren't what they used to be. I remember buying several John Deere mowers once for a job. I knew the company made great tractors, and I wanted something high quality and American made. The mowers turned out to be assembled in Mexico, as I recall, and they were junk. They didn't last long, either. I have had the same problem now with other companies that originally produced nothing but quality equipment. I suppose the original owner of the company died or sold out to some bigger corporation, and the bean counters decided that since they already had a great reputation, they could start cutting corners and get away with it.

I mention all this because with mowers these days, you won't automatically get what you pay for. It is entirely possible to buy a name-brand mower, pay a high price for it, and end up with a piece of junk. It's also possible to buy a very good, reasonably priced lawn mower.

So far I have heard good reports from most people about the mowers made by the Japanese motorcycle and carmakers. You'll also find some lawn mowers from the makers of chain saws, and hopefully their mowers are as good as their saws. I won't name names here, but there is a very popular magazine that ranks products—and from what I've seen, its advice on lawn mowers isn't worth a hoot. Of the American-made mowers, most mower repair people I know prefer to work on Briggs & Stratton engines; many swear that these are by far the best. I'm not sure that I'd argue with that assessment.

## Lawn Mower Safety

Each year more than seventy-four thousand small children, adolescents, and adults are injured by rotary, hand, and riding power mowers in the United States. Here's how to avoid becoming one of these statistics:

- Never pour gasoline into a hot engine. Gas could get on the very hot cooling fins and ignite.
- Never add gasoline to a lawn mower that's running. Always shut it down first.
- If you spill gasoline on the top of the mower while you're filling the tank, then clean it up with a rag or wait and let it evaporate before starting the mower.
- Never attempt to do repairs on a hot lawn mower engine. Let it cool down first.
- Never, ever stick your fingers underneath a rotary lawn mower while the motor is running. Turn it off first.
- Never run a lawn mower inside your garage or any building. The fumes are toxic and can quickly pollute the inside air.
- Do not touch the spark plug or spark plug connections while the mower is running. A good shock is in order if you do.
- Always disconnect the spark plug wire before working on the mower. If you're attempting to move or disconnect the blade, then it's by far the safest to actually remove the spark plug first. Many mowers will start when the blade is turned.
- A safety tip about lawn mower pull cords: When you first pull the cord on a cold lawn mower, a hard yank will sometimes lead to the cord kicking back on you. This can wrench your shoulder hard enough to sprain a muscle or tear a ligament. With a perfectly cold engine, it's best to first give just a little pull, or two half pulls. Then give it a regular hard pull. Lawn mowers seem to start quicker this way, too.
- Never tie down the dead man bar on the lawn mower. This is the safety bar you need to hold down to keep the engine

running. On some more expensive mowers, the dead man bar will not shut down the mower when released, but instead will stop movement of the blade. No matter what sort of mower you have, do not tie down the dead man bar. It's there for a purpose.

- If you're working with an electric lawn mower and accidentally mow off the cord—first, don't panic. Do not touch the live end of the wire! Go to the outlet and unplug the cord. The two pieces can then be spliced together and carefully taped up with black electrical tape. If you aren't sure exactly how to splice and tape electrical wire correctly, don't do it yourself. Take it to a neighbor who is mechanically inclined and ask him or her to show you how it's done. You could also take the whole cord to any auto mechanic, who could also quickly show you how to do this right. Pay attention and then next time it happens you'll know just what to do.
- Never mow a lawn when the grass is wet. A slippery lawn could lead to a serious accident. At any rate, mowing a wet lawn isn't good for the grass and can easily cause diseases. It's best not to even walk on your lawn when it's wet. Likewise, never walk on or mow a lawn that's covered with frost.
- Always look over the lawn for objects before you mow it. Rotary mowers in particular will pick up a rock, bolt, bottle, or any small, hard object and throw it with great force.
- Don't wear loose, dangling clothing while operating a power lawn mower. I know of one instance when a girl who was mowing a lawn wrapped a blanket around her shoulders to keep warm. The blanket got caught in the mower blade and almost instantly became wrapped so tight that the girl was strangled to death. Incidents like this are even more common with riding lawn mowers.

### Insider's Tip

Lawn mowers, no matter what kind, need to be kept where they are out of the elements. Leave any mower outside in the rain and snow, and it will quickly fall apart and soon be useless. Rainwater or dew will get inside the gas tank and will make the mower impossible to start. Even a nonmotorized lawn mower should be kept under cover, because moisture will quickly rust the blades.

## The Perfect Lawn Mower

Ever wonder what the perfect lawn mower would be?

I asked a woman I know what her idea of a perfect lawn mower was, and she said: "Five foot ten, 160 pounds, brown hair, brown eyes, strong, young, and cheap."

But hey, let's get serious here, right? There are plenty of good machines out there, but my advice is this: Own three lawn mowers. Ideally, you have a shed to keep a mower in. Why not have three of them? For someone with an average lawn or two to mow, three would be ideal. First would be a good, newer mulching rotary mower. Second is a backup rotary mower—an older model, but one that's easy to start. And third is a good nonmotorized push lawn mower.

Why have three? Well, sometimes even the best of mowers gets stubborn and just won't start. But suppose your lawn is getting tall, and today is the only day you have the time to mow the lawn. That's when the old backup mower comes in handy. For those crazy days when neither power mower will start, you get out the push mower and start mowing. You'll get plenty of exercise, but your lawn will get mowed.

It's necessary to keep your lawn mowed at regular intervals to keep it looking really nice. Sometimes in areas other than the Western United States, it rains for days on end during spring, summer, or fall. Suppose you were planning to mow your lawns on the weekend but all weekend it rains? Your lawns respond to the rain by growing even faster and taller. Now you *really* need to get them mowed, but the next weekend when it isn't raining, your lawn mower won't start. Again, this is where the backup mower comes in handy. And, if necessary, the backup to the backup. As long as you get the job done and the lawn mowed.

By the way, did you ever notice how fast your lawns grow after a big thunderstorm? There's a reason for this, besides all the extra water. The air contains 78 percent nitrogen. Nitrogen is the main element that encourages the fast growth of grasses. But the nitrogen in the air isn't normally available for plants to use. When lightning strikes, however, it fixes nitrogen in the air, converting it to ammonium form. The rain that falls during these storms is thus often rich with available nitrogen. Which makes the lawns grow like crazy, hence your need to get them mowed before they get totally out of hand.

## Buying a Good Used Lawn Mower

A word to the wise on finding a good secondhand power mower. Buy a used one from the want ads of your newspaper, and buy it off season. In the middle of summer, it's hard to find a good deal on a decent lawn mower, but when lawns are dormant, mowers are plentiful—and cheap, too. I've bought a number of perfectly good backup lawn mowers and have paid between fifteen and thirty dollars for them. A late-fall or early-wintertime garage sale is a perfect place for finding bargains on lawn mowers. If your town has a large number of college students who leave for the summer, then you can often find cheap mowers at garage sales the last weekend, right after finals are over.

Having that second power mower as a backup will pay dividends. Here's how to find a good one:

- Look in the local newspaper's want ads, and especially at garage sales.

- Go to garage sales early, before the best deals are gone.
- Certain brands of mowers are worth more than others. Don't expect to buy an almost new Toro or Honda mower for the same price as a bottom-of-the-line Sears model.
- Unhook the spark plug wire on the mower and pull the cord several times. There should be considerable stiff resistance. If the cord pulls out very easily, then there's a good chance the rings in the engine are badly worn. If this is the case, you don't want this mower.
- Check to see if the mower has gasoline in the tank. Refasten the spark plug wire and try to start the mower. Ideally, it will fire up and run on the first or second pull. If it takes more than three pulls to start, don't buy it.
- While the mower is running, take a look; is it smoking? A mower that smokes will burn oil and is probably about shot. If it smokes much at all, don't buy it.
- Shut off the mower. Take a good look at how the wheels are adjusted. See if you can adjust them; actually give it a try. Some of the cheapest mowers have wheels that require tools to adjust up or down. This is no plus. If the wheels are difficult to adjust but everything else is good, and the price is right—twenty bucks or so—consider buying it as a backup mower. If the mowing height is difficult to adjust and the owner wants forty dollars or more, forget it. Still . . . it's perfectly acceptable to bargain at garage sales. See if the owner will knock off some of the price.
- Give the wheels a shake and see if they're on solidly. Many lower-priced mowers have cheap wheels without ball bearings, and these will break and fall off. If the wheels are about to go, don't buy it.
- With lawn mowers, more horsepower is better than less. Expect to pay a little more for a good five- or six-horsepower mower than you would for a three-and-a-half-horsepower model. A larger engine means the mower won't have to work as hard. Larger engines often last longer.

## The Zen of Lawn Mower Maintenance

There is an incredible amount of BS written about maintaining your lawn mower. I read over and over again that you should sharpen your blades every month, or after every eight hours of mowing, and so on. But did you ever actually try this? Sharpening a lawn mower isn't like sharpening a chain saw; it's a whole lot harder. Many books show pictures of folks with their rotary mower blade in a vise while they sharpen the blade with a large file. First of all, it's darn hard to get one of these blades off the mower. If you even try this, you need to first make sure you unfasten the wire from the spark plug, because on some models turning that blade can start the engine!

I suggest this: If you're lucky enough to have a good lawn mower repair shop around that doesn't charge an arm and a leg, then once a year take your best mower in and have the folks there sharpen it. Do it during the off season if you can.

But sure, if you're handy with tools and like to do everything yourself, then by all means take off the blade (if you can!) and sharpen it with a large, flat file. What dulls a lawn mower blade more than anything else is hitting rocks, bricks, or dirt. If you're mowing an area where large tree roots stick up high enough to hit with the blades, watch out for these, too. If you hit an object that simply won't move, you're going to break something fast. Many mowers have a shear pin that's supposed to break before the engine does, but these often don't work. I've seen plenty of lawn mowers that were killed dead when the operator nailed a really stout tree root with them. This is one of the reasons you might want to think twice before you lend your mower to the kid next door. Last time I did that was the last time that one ever ran.

What is the number one thing to do to keep your lawn mower running? Check the oil! Most mowers have a little screw cap that you twist open to check the oil. You should open this up and check the oil *before* you start the mower, every time. Try to get in the habit of doing this, so that it just becomes second nature. The surest way to ruin a motor is to run it low on oil. If you are unsure of what exact kind of oil to use, just add some of the same kind of oil you'd put in the engine of your car. Regular thirty-weight motor oil should be just fine.

## LAWN MOWER PULL CORDS

Here's a tip that's well worth the price of this book all by itself! Many newer pull-start power lawn mowers have a rubber "stop" on the cord to keep you from pulling out the cord too far. Often this rubber stop will break and fall off with use. If this happens, take some black electrical tape and wrap it around the cord tightly, in the same spot that the stop used to be. Wrap enough tape in this spot so that it is impossible to pull the cord any farther than the stop. If you overpull a starter cord, you'll probably bust the cord recoil—the rewind unit. Then the cord won't wind back up again and you'll have to take it down to the repair shop. Don't even bother to try to repair one of these recoil units yourself. It will probably drive you half crazy if you try.

If you buy a used mower that doesn't have a stop on the pull cord, figure out how far you need to pull the cord in order to start the machine. Then, using the black tape method described above, put a new stop on the cord. This will save you a world of trouble. After a year or less, the tape may get soft and start to move downward on the cord as you pull on it. If this happens, get out some new tape and replace the old material. Whatever you do, do yourself a favor and don't pull out your recoil unit.

## WINTERIZING YOUR LAWN MOWERS

The day you park your mowers for the winter (assuming you don't live in Florida, California, or Arizona) is a good time to do some very basic maintenance work.

- Toward the end of the lawn mowing season, start using up most of the gasoline you have in your gas can. You really don't want to keep this over winter, because moisture may form in the can and dilute the gas. If you still have some gasoline left at the end of the season, make sure you keep the can indoors. You also want to use a standard red or orange gas can. I like the heavy plastic ones the best since they don't rust.

- Start up your mower and mow your lawn for the last time of the year. Try to burn up most of the gasoline in the tank. Do not replace it.
- Remove the gas cap. If there's still a considerable amount of gas in the tank, put the gas cap back on, restart the mower, and let it idle until most of the gas is used up. Let the engine cool down for at least ten minutes and then tip the mower on its side and drain out any old gasoline into a pan. Pour this old gas in an empty plastic gallon or half-gallon jug and put the top on it. An empty Clorox jug works well for this.
- Remove the cap where you check the oil. While the engine is still warm, tip the mower on its side and drain out the old motor oil into a pan. Put the oil in the same plastic gallon jug you used for your old leftover gasoline. You can take this down to a gas station later, and the staff will add it to their used oil tank for you. Never run old oil or gas down a drain—it'll find its way into local creeks and kill off the fish. Replace the old oil with fresh, new motor oil and put the cap back on. Do *not* forget to replace the old oil with new!
- Once the engine has cooled down, take out the air filter. If it's cardboard, blow it clean with an air hose. Use the air hose down at the gas station if you don't own an air compressor. If the air filter is made of foam, wire, or mesh, clean it in some gasoline and let it dry out before you replace it. If you can't even find the air cleaner, have the lawn mower repair people clean or replace it for you. But have them show you where it is and how to remove it, so that next time you can do it yourself.
- Remove the spark plug. Take the old plug with you to the lawn mower repair shop, buy a new one, and replace it yourself. If you don't have a socket and ratchet, you can buy a kit with these tools for very little money; they're pretty much

essential tools to own, too. You should have one large and longer-than-normal socket for removing spark plugs. A good spark plug socket will have a rubber damper in the top to protect the ceramic ends of the plugs.

- Using a wire brush, clean up the bottom of the mower. Clean off all old grass. If your mower is a typical air-cooled machine, check to see if there is any old grass stuck on the cooling fins. If so, clean these up, too.
- A few larger lawn mowers are now water cooled. If your mower has a radiator, check the fluid levels. If you have straight water in the radiator, drain it now and then replace it with fresh water, to which you should add 50 percent antifreeze.
- If your mower has an electric starting motor, but it's not an electric mower, now is the time to check the battery terminals for corrosion. If there is any, remove the cables and then clean the posts with a stiff brush or a pocketknife. If you leave the cables disconnected over winter, the battery will last longer.
- Now is a good time to consider sharpening the mower blade(s). Easiest by far is to just take it to the pros and have them do it for you. This shouldn't cost more than about fifteen dollars. Expect to pay more for sharpening reel-type and riding lawn mowers.
- To winterize an electric lawn mower, just unplug it and park it in the garage. Low maintenance is one of the best features of electric mowers.

## Beyond Mowing: Edging Your Lawn

While just about everyone mows, if you want a really top-notch, first-class lawn, you'll need to edge it. You don't see the same number of lawn edgers being used today as you used to. When I was a boy, everyone edged their lawns right after they mowed. Today, sadly, this is less common. A good job of edging sets off a nice lawn, making its borders look sharper, cleaner.

There are a number of good tools to use for edging lawns, and each has its advocates. Each has its advantages and disadvantages, too.

### GAS-POWERED EDGERS

These are small, motorized edgers that you walk behind and push. The blade, which is in the front of the machine, is kept at a slight angle and uses the edge of the sidewalk as a cutting board for trimming the grass. An edger like this, in the right hands, can do a beautiful job. With a less experienced operator, the results are sometimes less impressive.

The engines on these gas edgers are smaller, often three horsepower. Engines on edgers have all the same problems as do engines on power lawn mowers. All the advice listed above under lawn mower maintenance would also apply.

The main advantages of these edgers are that they can do a very effective job yet are fairly easy to use. The biggest disadvantage is that the front blade wears down and needs to be repaired frequently if much edging is done. Another disadvantage is that you pretty much need cement walkways to edge against.

### WEED WHIPS OR STRING TRIMMERS

Many people now use their weed whip to edge their lawns. Weed whips, which use fishing line to cut grass, are fairly easy to use, but doing a really good job of edging with them isn't always that simple. The big advantage with a weed whip is that you don't need a smooth concrete walkway or sidewalk to do effective edging. With a whip, you can edge the lawn where it wants to wander off into the flower beds. You can edge it where it's bordered with rocks or a fence. A weed whip is extremely versatile, and no doubt this is why they have become so popular.

There are also electric string-type edgers, with or without cords, that work perfectly well for edging. My experience with battery-operated edgers hasn't been good. They lack the power of a plug-in model. You also need to drag a long cord around and have to be careful not to cut it. But still, these are inexpensive and well worth considering.

Most of the gas-powered string edgers use a fuel mix of gasoline and oil. You'll need to mix this blend exactly according to the instructions, and you'll need to keep the fuel in its own separate, well-labeled gas can. You don't want to run one of these on straight gas or you'll quickly ruin the engine. Likewise, you don't want to accidentally put this fuel in your gasoline-powered lawn mower; you could foul out the spark plug and maybe gum up your carburetor.

### *Insider's Tip*

Never run a weed whip or any kind of string trimmer, gas or electric, without wearing some protection for your eyes! Safety glasses or a safety face shield are by far the best. At the very least, wear a solid pair of wraparound sunglasses. String trimmers will throw small rocks and throw them hard. It's a good idea to wear a long-sleeved shirt, too, to save yourself some bruises.

### HAND EDGERS

Mowing a lawn is only the first step. No lawn can look really fabulous unless it is well edged. A nice job of edging gives any lawn clean, sharp boundaries. If you hire someone to mow your lawns, insist that they be edged, too. It ought to be part of the package, and in days past it always was. However, I notice more and more lawns being maintained now by "mow, blow, and go" gardeners who don't bother to edge. Insist on edging!

Hand edgers have the one great advantage that all nonmotorized tools enjoy: They always start! You don't need to check their oil, add gasoline, or plug them in; you just pick them up and go to work. Handtools are also safer to use, and a whole lot quieter, too. They're environmentally friendly and don't add to air pollution.

- **Barn scrapers.** If you can find one of these at a farm auction or farm supply store, it'll make a pretty good lawn edger. The best barn scrapers have a flat blade on the end of a straight, long, wooden handle. The original use of this tool was for scraping cow poop off cement barn walkways. To use one, just set the blade next to the edge of the lawn, as close to the sidewalk as possible, and then step down on the topside of the blade.

- **Step-on hand edgers.** These look sort of like a hoe, except that the blade is rounded and points straight down. You place the edger next to the sidewalk and step down on the flat part above the blade. Your weight pushes the blade down and trims the grass. These will work all right if they're kept sharp, but they're less effective without a cement walkway to edge against. This type of edger seems to be making a comeback. They are inexpensive to buy, safe, and easy to use.

- **Flat-ended nursery spades.** If you happen to own a really good straight-shanked nursery spade, consider yourself lucky! You can buy these with a flat bottom edge that's ribbed for extra cutting ability. I don't even want to call this tool a "shovel," since it's so much better. I like a nursery spade with a long handle and a long, straight blade. A nursery spade will quickly become the most useful garden tool you own. Look in the Resources section of this book for places to find a good one.

- **Rotary wheel hand-push edgers.** These are the old-fashioned edgers you used to see all over. A brand-new one will work fairly well, but an older, dull one isn't much fun. You can sometimes buy an old one at a garage sale for a dollar or two, and it'll be better than no edger, but not much.

- **The Edge Hound.** This newer tool is very similar to a barn scraper, and it works just as well or better. It's made by Hound Dog Products in Minnesota. This company also makes another hand edger called the Steppin' Edger, and this, too, is easy to use and works fine.

The Edge Hound will do a pretty good job of edging, but it does require some effort. I weigh more than two hundred pounds, so when I step down on one of these, something happens. If you are considerably lighter than I am, you'll probably find the Steppin' Edger, with its slimmer blade, easier to use. Both of these tools are solidly made and ought to last for many years.

CHAPTER 7

# How to Mow a Lawn

There are really no hard-and-fast rules to follow about mowing lawns. Still, there are some things you can keep in mind that will result in healthier, better-looking lawns. The following are a basic dozen tips for the best way to mow your lawn.

- **Never mow the lawn too short.** Check the mowing charts in appendix C for each species of grass and make sure you don't mow your own grass lower than it should be cut. If in doubt, mow a little bit higher. The old "one-third rule" is a good one: Never cut off more than a third of the height of the grass.

- **The more often you mow, the better.** Most lawns will do all right if they're mowed once a week during the growing season, but if they were mowed twice a week, it would be even better. If you can help it, never let the grass get too high before you mow. This way, you never remove too much of the leaf blades at any one time. It's much easier on the lawn.

- **A sharp lawn mower will always cut better than a dull one.** If it's too difficult to sharpen the blade(s) yourself (as it often is), then at least once a season take the mower to a repair shop and pay to have it sharpened. Dull blades rip off the grass, leaving jagged edges that look bad and are more susceptible to fungal diseases.

- **Never mow your lawn when it's wet.** Wait until the lawn is dry on the surface before mowing it. Lawns that are mowed wet will not cut as well, and they'll look unkempt; mowing wet grass is also a great way to spread lawn diseases.

- **Don't import trouble.** If you borrow a mower from someone who has a weedy lawn, there will almost certainly be weed seeds all over and under it. Be sure to clean the entire mower with a stiff broom before you mow your own grass. If you hire people to mow your lawn, ask them to clean the mower before they start. This is a good defense against importing noxious things like crabgrass seeds.
- **Lawn mowers always cut grass best at medium speeds.** If you push the mower too slow or too fast, it won't cut as well. Experiment a bit and find just the right speed where it seems to cut the best, then try to stick to that speed as much as possible. On very thick lawns, slow down a little and mow slower.
- **Even the best of lawn mowers will miss some grass.** It's always a good idea to go back over the lawn you've just mowed and recut any spots that look less than perfect. For a really perfect-looking cut, wait an hour or two so that uncut, bent-over grass has time to stand back up. Then go back over any odd spots and mow them again.
- **Be careful with clippings.** In areas where there's a lot of damp, cloudy, or rainy weather, it's a good idea to bag or rake up the grass clippings so they don't encourage fungal diseases. If you're in an area where the weather is warm and dry, however, it usually makes sense to leave the clippings on the lawn after you've mowed. Anytime you leave clippings on the lawn, though, you should take a good look at them. Are some of the clippings in piles or thick rows? If this is the case, rake up any area where the clippings are too thick. A thin, even layer of clippings is good; thick piles of fresh lawn clippings can smother the grass underneath.
- **Don't mow the lawn in the same direction each time.** If one week you mow in straight lines from north to south, try mowing it the next time in lines going from east to west. If you always mow the lawn in straight lines, once in a while mow it in large circles instead. Certain types of grasses seem to have a "mowing memory," and if they're always mowed in the same direction, they start to look odd after a while.

- **Try mowing a checkerboard.** For that pattern you see on some professional baseball fields, mow one row very straight in one direction, north to south or south to north. Next, skip an entire row of lawn the width of your lawn mower. Keep doing this until you have all the lawn half mowed. Now come at the lawn from the opposite direction, east to west or west to east, and mow, again skipping an entire row with each pass. If you do it right, the end result is a lawn with that interesting checkerboard pattern.

  If you really want to get serious about this business of mowing in checkerboards, mow one directional section of it one day. Wait a day and then mow the next section from the other direction. This is what's being done on some of those pro baseball fields. It's a good bit of work, but the lawn looks pretty interesting when you're done.

- **Don't try to cut as much grass as possible with every pass.** Overlap each pass of the mower by several inches or more. If your mower can cut a twenty-two-inch swath, then try actually just cutting about an eighteen-inch swath with each pass. The thicker your lawn, the more you should overlap onto the area just cut. This overlapping will result in a much better-looking cut and is a good way to keep from missing some spots altogether.

- **Be safe while you're mowing the lawn.** Use common sense. Keep kids and pets away from any power equipment. Look over the lawn before you mow it; if you see any toys, rocks, pieces of wood, or hard objects, remove them before you start. Keep your fingers out from under any power lawn mowers, and if you need to clean or unplug a mower, turn if off first. If you need to add more gasoline, move the mower well off the lawn. Any gas you spill on the lawn will result in dead grass. Lastly, keep the safety of any trees in your lawn in mind, too. A young tree's protective bark can easily be permanently damaged if someone keeps running into it with the side or front of a lawn mower. Give your lawn trees a break.

For more advice on mowing lawns, please see appendix C.

# PART THREE
# Problem Lawns

CHAPTER 8

# Fixing Up an Existing Lawn

*I*n this chapter on lawn repair, you'll see that there is a good deal of necessary overlapping of advice. Much of what you'll find here would also apply to starting a lawn from scratch. If you're starting a brand-new lawn on bare soil, it would still be worthwhile for you to read this section on basic lawn fixes.

## Repairing Bad Spots in a Lawn

If you have a lawn that is in pretty good condition overall, but has a few spots where the grass just doesn't grow, then just repair these spots rather than reworking the entire lawn.

Sometimes you'll have spots where nothing will grow—no grass, no weeds even. This may well be a spot where you spilled some gasoline while filling up your lawn mower, or perhaps it's the place your (or your neighbor's!) dog always stops to pee.

With a shovel, dig out the top three inches of soil and remove it. Replace this soil with some dirt from another part of your yard. Make sure the soil you've added is level with the existing soil of the lawn. Steal some topsoil from one of your flower beds if you need to. Rake this new soil smooth, sprinkle a tiny bit of high-nitrogen fertilizer on the spot, rake the fertilizer in, and then reseed the spot. You can also use a handful of bonemeal or blood meal as fertilizer if you don't like using chemicals. Remember, though, that dogs are attracted to bonemeal and will often tear up the spot looking for the lost "bone."

If you live in the North and have a bluegrass lawn, use blended bluegrass seed. If you live out West and have a fescue lawn, use a fescue blend. Try to use the seed that matches your lawn the closest. Cover the seed with a light dusting of steer manure, about a quarter inch deep. The birds will probably eat any seed you don't cover. Lightly tamp down the covered seed with the palm of your hand.

Sometimes you can simply go down to a local nursery and buy a small piece of sod to use as a replacement. This works great—providing it's the same kind of grass as your lawn.

If you have a hybrid Bermuda, Saint Augustine, or centipede grass lawn, you can always go to the far side and dig up a few small plugs of grass (with roots!) to plug into the new patch. They should quickly spread and fill in the spot.

Keep the newly repaired spots moist for a week or so, and in no time you should be back in business. Once in a rare while you'll encounter a spot where the above method won't work. Sometimes the grass will start to grow quite well and then suddenly die. Usually this is because the soil is polluted there far deeper than the three inches you replaced. In this case, you'll need to redo the whole thing, digging down deeper this time. On a few occasions, I have seen bad spots in a lawn that were directly over a large broken drain tile. All the water in these spots drained off so fast that the grass above it invariably dried out before the rest of the lawn. If this turns out to be the case, then dig down and remove the tile, or plug it up.

### *Insider's Tip*

There are patches sold now, such as the Scotts PatchMaster, that already have seed, fertilizer, and mulch all in one pad. You just put the pad down, water it, and it will grow. If you use one of these seed pads, make sure it has the same kind of grass as your lawn, or the results will look odd.

No matter whether you use sod, seed, plugs, or a patch, you still need to keep the area moist enough for the repair to take hold and grow in. For the first two weeks, you don't want this spot to get dry at all. If you used seed, you need only lightly sprinkle the spot. If plugs or sod were used, you'll need to give the whole area a decent soaking.

Avoid using any herbicides on these new patches of lawn for at least several months. Herbicides can easily kill new grasses. If any weeds do sprout in these new areas, pull them out by hand while they're small. Try to avoid stepping on these spots, too. Give them a chance, and pretty soon they should be blended right back into your lawn.

## Overseeding

With cool-season lawns, you can sometimes do a darn good job of repair simply by overseeding the entire lawn. Mow the lawn as short as possible and bag or rake up the clippings. Sprinkle two pounds of actual nitrogen fertilizer over the entire area (see chapter 4), reseed the lawn with the same sort of grass that is already growing there, cover it all about a quarter inch deep with steer manure, and start watering it. For the first ten days, try to keep the soil surface uniformly moist. Any seed you can still see will need to be covered lightly with manure. Don't bother to try to water deeply at this point; just keep the top inch moist to get the seed germinating. Seed that starts to grow and then dries out will quickly die.

Don't mow this reseeded lawn for about three weeks after seeding. The first time you mow it, set your mower so that you only cut off only an inch or so of the grass. Don't mow it too low.

The first four or five times you mow a newly reseeded lawn, make sure to use a catcher on your lawn mower, because the clippings can smother the newly emerging grass seedlings. If your mower doesn't have a catcher, then rake up the clippings as soon as you've finished mowing. Several months after you've reseeded, you can lower the blades on your mower a bit; this is a good time to refertilize the new, revitalized lawn. At this point, you can go back to using the mulching mower, or to just leaving the clippings behind if you're using a reel-type mower.

A few words about watering the lawn: In general, the rule of thumb (except when you're trying to get new seed to sprout and grow) is that it's far better to soak your lawns than to just sprinkle them. Deep watering encourages deep roots, and this makes the whole lawn stronger. Deep roots can reach more water during dry periods, and they can also tap into more nutrient reserves in the soil. You're better soaking most lawns for an hour every three or four days in summer than you would be to sprinkle a little each day.

As with all rules, there are a few exceptions to this watering rule. In desert areas in the middle of summer, the best lawns are kept green with a combination of deep soaking and light watering. In Las Vegas or Phoenix, for example, it's common practice to soak the lawn one day and then sprinkle it for at least seven or eight minutes once or even twice a day on the days between the soakings.

Heavy clay soil may not be able to soak up as much water as it needs before the water starts to run off. In this case, it's necessary to soak until the water starts to run off, then turn it off, let it soak in for an hour or so, and resume soaking. With lawns that are growing on steep slopes, it may also be necessary to do the soaking in a series of steps.

The bottom line with the watering of all plants is that when they're dry, apply some water. Keep in mind, too, that when it's hot and windy all plants, lawns included, will dry out much faster than normally.

## OVERSEEDING WARM-WEATHER LAWNS IN WINTER

Many Southern-type lawns—Bermuda, zoysia, buffalo grass, and the like—will go completely dormant with the first hard frost in fall, and stay dormant until late the next spring. Some gardeners like the look of the brown, dormant lawn, but others of us are less fond of it.

These dormant lawns can be overseeded each fall with a cool-season lawn grass that will grow all winter long, and will provide that lush green look even when the weather is cold. The safest grass to use for this wintertime color is annual ryegrass, although many people use bluegrass seed or perennial ryegrass seed.

### *Insider's Tip*

If you're using perennial grass seed, there is a little trick well worth remembering. In springtime, just as the weather is starting to warm up and you'd expect the dormant warm-season grass to come out of its winter dormancy, mow the lawn very short. Then immediately apply some fertilizer that is high in nitrogen. A very short mowing right now will rob the winter grass of energy and permit the summer grass to come on through.

When you want to overseed a dormant winter lawn, first you mow the dormant lawn as short as you can get it, then apply some fertilizer with nitrogen in it. I like to use nitrate of soda or ammonium nitrate fertilizers for this job, since both work better than most when the weather is cool. Then seed. If you're using annual ryegrass seed, sprinkle on around ten pounds per thousand square feet of lawn. With bluegrass, use four pounds per thousand; with perennial rye, use five to seven pounds. Sometimes people use a fifty-fifty mix of annual and perennial ryegrass seed for this overseeding.

Cover the seed with a quarter to half an inch of steer manure and keep it all sprinkled so that the manure mulch stays uniformly moist for the first two weeks. This will often require three or four short irrigations a day if the weather is sunny or windy.

Set the blades on your lawn mower much higher than you'd normally mow. You want to mow this winter lawn two to three inches high to keep it looking good. Be sure to use a catcher on the mower for the first several mowings of the winter-seeded lawn.

The bottom line on overseeding lawns is that it's generally a good idea and can be done yearly. Any lawn that is getting thin in spots can generally be improved by adding some seed, fertilizer, and manure.

## Renovation

Normally when we talk about renovating a lawn, we're talking about a fairly major overhaul. If your lawn looks pretty good and you just wish it were thicker and greener, then aerating, fertilizing, and reseeding will probably work just fine. But if your lawn is a mess, it might be time to renovate.

If you have a thatch-building lawn—Saint Augustine, Bermuda grass, zoysia, bent grass, centipede grass, or even Kentucky bluegrass—sooner or later you'll probably need to dethatch it. Thatch is a thick layer of living and dead stems, roots, rhizomes, plant crowns, and other plant parts that develop between the layer of green vegetation and the soil surface. This thatch layer is plant residue in various stages of decay. Thatch accumulation occurs when the rate of thatch production is greater than the rate of decay. Grasses vary in the rate in which they develop thatch layers.

Certain things you do will encourage the growth of thatch. Using too much nitrogen fertilizer will over time contribute to it. Watering often and never deeply will promote thatch. Mowing a lawn infrequently and then leaving the clippings on will add to it. Using a side-discharge rotary lawn mower without a bagger will add to thatch buildup, especially if the lawn is mowed infrequently. Thatch buildup is also encouraged by excessively high mowing (greater than three inches) and vigorous grass cultivars. Factors that slow decay include high soil acidity, heavy clay soils, poor drainage, reduced soil insect activity, and reduced levels of beneficial soil fungi and bacteria.

High-maintenance lawns with rapidly growing grass varieties and heavy fertilization programs are likely to develop thick layers of thatch. Thatch buildup is often described as a "disease of good lawns." Excessive thatch accumulation (greater than half an inch deep) creates conditions that may well result in the deterioration of the lawn. Thick thatch leads to reduced water and fertilizer infiltration into the soil. This in turn will result in less resistance to drought, reduced rooting of the individual grass plants, increased sensitivity to temperature and moisture extremes, problems with the performance of lawn pesticides, and in general increased susceptibility to insect and disease problems.

The general quality of a lawn declines as thatch buildup occurs. A lawn with thick thatch will not respond well to fertilizer applications or irrigation, and is easily damaged by stressful conditions such as drought, high heat, severe cold, predatory insects, or fungal lawn diseases.

## *Insider's Tip*

Thatch prevention can be managed by judicious use of fertilizers and pesticides and by good cultural practices. Keeping the soil pH between 6 and 7 encourages microbe and earthworm activity. Selecting grass species that do not normally form thatch will also prevent and reduce the rate of thatch buildup. Mowing grass regularly at correct heights (usually two to two and a half inches) can also help slow thatch buildup.

Topdressing, in which a thin layer of soil (one-eighth to one-quarter inch) is added to the lawn, is a good preventive measure for slowing thatch buildup. The light dusting of soil helps improve the environment on the soil surface and encourages microbial activity. The best soil to use is well-matured compost, or any good silty or loamy soil. Adding peat moss isn't a good idea—this will just add to the thatch. Topdressing should not be added on top of an already existing thatch layer.

Because thatch is fibrous, it's quite high in carbon, and high-carbon materials tie up nitrogen. A lawn with deep thatch is often starved for fertilizer, but adding more nitrogen to a thatch-built-up lawn only encourages the growth of even more thatch.

Because thatch sits under the grass, it's the perfect spot for molds to grow. Sometimes molds or other fungi that grow in thatch will spread to the lawn itself and kill off parts of it. But a more common problem with thatch is that it provides an ideal place for mold spores to grow. A deep layer of thatch can easily contribute to a much higher-than-normal mold spore count in the area over and around the lawn. This is yet one more reason for removing thatch.

### *Insider's Tip*

If you use a power dethatcher, it's a good idea to wear a paper face mask while you're running it, and also afterward while you're raking up all that chopped-up thatch. When you're finished with this job, take a nice long shower and shampoo your hair, washing away all the mold spores and dirt.

As thatch builds up, the lawn itself gets higher and higher than the walkways to its sides. I have seen lawns that were almost five inches above the sidewalks! Originally these lawns were even with the sidewalks, but over time the thatch built up higher and higher, pushing the lawn up with it.

If you have an inch or less of thatch, you can probably correct the problem by hand-raking and aerating. Go over the entire lawn with a stiff iron garden rake and rake up as much thatch as you can. You'll pull up plenty of nice grass as you do this, but do it anyhow. (You'll also get a serious workout!) Bag up all the grass and thatch you've raked up and then aerate the lawn with an aerator. Once this is done, you'll want to add fertilizer, a little mulch, and then just water it. Most thatch-building lawns have plenty of underground stems; once the thatch is removed and fertilizer, air, light, and water are applied, these lawns will usually take off and grow like mad.

But if your lawn has that serious, spongy-to-walk-on, deep thatch buildup, you have a much bigger job ahead of you. You'll need to rent a power dethatcher—also called a power knife, a vertical cutter, or a power rake. Generally power dethatchers cost a bit more per hour to rent than do power lawn aerators. Expect to pay around twelve dollars an hour to rent one.

### *Insider's Tip*

Before you use a dethatcher, mow your lawn with a power rotary lawn mower that has a bagger on it. Set the mower so that it will cut at the lowest possible level. Remove as much grass as possible before you start the dethatching.

Power dethatching units are quite heavy and fairly difficult to work with. They have blades or knives that cut through the lawn and thatch into the soil below. Ideally, you'll want the blades to cut about half an inch into the actual soil. Dethatcher blades can be adjusted so that you can cut down as deep as needed, but no deeper. This is one job that really might be best hired out. But then, if you're strong and ambitious, why not give it a try? You'll save some money and get one fine, hard, sweaty workout for sure.

The blades on a dethatcher can also be adjusted for width. You can set them as close as an inch or as far as three inches apart on most units. If you have a coarse-bladed lawn such as Bermuda grass, you'll want the blades closer together. The finer the lawn type (bluegrass, bent grasses), the farther apart you should set the blades. It's a good idea to ask the dealer to adjust the blades for you before you take the machine home. Many of these machines are very difficult to adjust—some are next to impossible.

Run the power dethatcher over the entire lawn several times, approaching it from different directions so that you get a crossover and overlapping effect. When you're finished, get out the heavy rakes and rake up all of the chopped-up thatch and grass.

### AFTER DETHATCHING

Once you've dethatched the lawn and cleaned up the mess, then what? Now's the time to spread the fertilizer, sprinkle on some grass seed, cover the seed with a thin layer of steer manure, and water it all thoroughly. If you live east of the Mississippi River, your soil is probably acidic; or you may have done a soil test and know that it's acidic. If this is the case, then now is also a good time to spread some dolomite lime on your lawn. Use around five pounds of lime for every hundred square feet of lawn (ten-by-ten-foot area).

Remember, a lawn that has just been dethatched has been worked over pretty hard, and it will need plenty of water for several weeks afterward. Also, a newly dethatched lawn will look pretty rough, but sometimes in order to get something beautiful, we need to do whatever it takes.

## Reestablishment

Much of the advice in this section on reestablishment of an existing lawn will also apply to anyone simply starting a new lawn. There is a good deal of natural overlap here in the best practices used.

*Starting all over* we might call this, since this is what we do when we just flat-out give up on the lawn we have. Say your lawn is made up of five or six different types of grass plus a liberal assortment of broadleaf weeds. You might well decide it's time for this lawn to go. A lawn that's pretty much all weeds, common Bermuda and crabgrass, would be a good candidate for this extreme action.

Still, if your lawn is composed mostly of one kind of grass and seems at all repairable, try the above methods before you resort to this.

Reestablishment is a task normally best done in springtime or early summer. You need to be able to give the new lawn plenty of active growing time to get established before winter sets in. Exceptions might be in very hot-summer areas such as Phoenix, Arizona, where they start growing their spring materials in fall. In Phoenix, wintertime is the very best growing season of the year.

To totally renovate a lawn, you'll first need to kill off all the existing grass. The easiest way to do this, by far, is to buy a broad-spectrum herbicide such as Roundup and spray your entire lawn. Roundup has the chemical glyphosate as its main ingredient, and when you buy this or another herbicide, look to see what percentage of glyphosate is in the container. Use the more powerful stuff. Glyphosate will kill grasses and weeds from top to bottom, roots included. If it rains soon after you apply it, however, it won't be as effective. Glyphosate works quickly but is not known to persist in the soil. Supposedly, it breaks down quickly.

Wait an entire week after spraying the lawn with Roundup and check whether it looks dead or not. It's very possible that certain spots will still be alive; you'll need to respray these. After two weeks your lawn should be a goner. If you have a rotary lawn mower with a bagger, adjust the wheels so that you can mow it as low as possible. Mow and remove as much of the dead grass as you can.

Be darn careful *not* to get any of this spray on any other nearby plants. Don't get it on yourself, either. If it's a windy day, don't spray. Wait until it's dead calm.

Another, slower way to kill off your grass is to cover the entire lawn with a large sheet of black plastic. Tuck the corners in well, then leave the plastic in place for several weeks. If the weather is warm, the lawn should be dead by then.

There is another method you can try: Rent a sod cutter and simply remove the sod in strips. The problem with this is that if you have a grass that will regrow from roots or underground stems (rhizomes or stolons), such as Bermuda grass, then even removing the sod doesn't necessarily mean you've gotten rid of it all.

Once you've killed off your entire lawn, there are a number of ways to get started with a new one. First, though, you'll probably want to get rid of all the dead grass. You can dig it all under with a shovel, but this is mighty tedious work. It would be simpler to run over it several times with a dethatcher, then rake up the old grass. Some people run a rototiller right over the killed lawn, at some point using an iron rake to remove most of the old sod. Many landscapers simply work the rest of the dead grass back into the soil with the tiller. If you do this, it will add a certain amount of extra organic matter.

Another way to get rid of the old sod is to use a power edger. Lower the blade so that it cuts into the sod about an inch deep. Run the edger up and down the lawn, making long cuts across it. Cut the lawn in both directions so that eventually you have lots of rectangular pieces. Get under these pieces of sod with a flat-tipped garden spade, cut them out, and lift them out of the lawn area. If you have a compost heap, toss all of this into the heap.

### ROTOTILLING

A rototiller is a gas-powered machine with strong metal tines that tear up the soil. Some models have the tines in the front, others in the back. In either case, if you pass over soil a number of times with a rototiller, the soil is usually busted up pretty well. This is the main reason to use a rototiller: to break up the soil to the point that it's loose, friable, and easy to work with.

Several days before you intend to rototill, be sure to soak the lawn area thoroughly and deeply. Failure to soak the lawn ahead of time will usually mean that the soil is too hard and dry to till up well. Do not even consider rototilling soil that is still wet—you'll create thousands of small bricklike dirt clods and basically destroy any soil structure you might have had.

## *Insider's Tip*

This can be important information for some folks: If you have a tree growing in the middle of your lawn, it might well have a mass of shallow roots growing just under the soil surface. If this is the case and you start running the rototiller at all close to the tree, you'll be cutting hundreds of roots in half. By the time you've rototilled the soil well, it will look like a tornado went through it. Pieces of tree root will be sticking up everywhere, half chopped off and half still attached. To get rid of these, you'll need to go around with an ax or very sharp spade and chop every single one of them off. This can add a huge amount of time and effort to the job—and in many instances, it isn't worth all the effort involved.

If you encounter this kind of situation, consider planting ground cover around the base of the tree instead of lawn. Also consider not rototilling that part of the old lawn area at all. Just let it go. It would be a good idea to go over it with a power aerator, but forget trying to rototill areas like this.

Large rototillers can be rented at rental yards, usually for about the same price per day as an aerator. Smaller rototillers will do the job, but they're much slower. As I've mentioned, rototillers come in either front-tine or rear-tine versions; the one you want to rent is the rear-tine tiller, which is much easier to use and more effective. The best rototillers I've ever used were English-made machines called Howard Gems. These are big tillers, plenty heavy, but they certainly do bust up the soil.

Once you have the old lawn torn up—and before you get too carried away with the rototiller—now is the best time to spread some complete fertilizer. Then spread an inch of steer manure over the entire area. If you have a large compost heap and lots of good, finished compost, add a layer of this to the soil, too. If your soil is acidic (below 6.5 pH), it's time to spread some dolomite limestone. Use six to seven pounds of lime per hundred square feet of soil.

If you live in a desert area and know for a fact that your soil is alkaline (7.5 or higher pH), then this is a good time to add some soil sulfur. Buy this material in large sacks at a farm supply store. Apply five pounds of soil sulfur for every hundred square feet.

If your soil is hard, sticky clay, it will benefit from a heavy application of gypsum. Gypsum adds calcium to the soil and will help soften up hard clays. Buy the gypsum from a masonry and cement yard, and get the kind that builders use for stucco walls. You can buy "soil gypsum" or "garden gypsum" at a nursery, but it's the same exact product. The only difference is that it will cost five times more at the nursery! Apply the gypsum liberally, ten pounds to every hundred square feet. It's almost impossible to apply too much gypsum to a Western, adobe clay soil.

Now that you have all the goodies over the top of the soil, start running the rototiller. If you have allergies or are the slightest bit sensitive to dust, wear a paper face mask while you start working all this material into the soil.

Work the tiller back and forth, then change directions so that you're crisscrossing where you've been already. Don't try to get too deep with your first passes with the tiller. Each time you go over the ground, it'll dig in a little bit deeper. On old lawns, even the best tillers want to jump right over certain extra-hard spots. It may be necessary to first bust up these hard spots with a pick.

Run the tiller until you have the entire lawn area nicely tilled up. Hopefully you will have worked the soil at least six inches deep. You really don't need to go much deeper than this. If your soil is sandy, you'll find the tilling to be fast and fairly easy. Loam soil will go a bit slower, and clay soils will take far longer.

Once your soil is all rototilled and the tiller is back at the rental yard, rake out the lawn until it's smooth and even. There are professional rakes made for this purpose, known as landscape rakes. If you can, rent one when you rent the tiller.

What makes a landscape rake special is that it's very wide, with many teeth. You can also nail a board onto the end of a long two-by-four and drag this along, using it as a rake and a leveler. What you want is a soil surface that is free of clumps, rocks, and other junk, and one that's level. If rainwater has a tendency to run toward your house, gently slope the surface of the soil away from the house. Also, make sure there are no high spots or low spots. In a lawn, high spots will dry out too fast and will get scalped by the mowers. Low spots will stay soggy and will have poor aeration. Try to get it as level as possible.

### ROLLERS

It's time to pass over your lawn once or twice with a roller. This is a large metal drum with an attached handle; you just drag it behind you to firm up the soil. Some models allow you to add water to give the roller more weight—but don't bother. Drag the roller behind you instead of pushing it, so that there will be fewer footmarks left. You can generally rent a roller at the same nursery where you buy the seed and manure. Often they'll just lend it to you free of charge if you promise to get it back to them quickly.

If you'll be seeding it, a leveled and rolled lawn will ideally be about half an inch lower than nearby sidewalks. If the soil is at the same level as or above the sidewalk, you may need to either remove some soil or go over it again with the roller—or perhaps both.

If you're planning to lay new sod on this soil, then you want the surface to be about one and a half inches below the surrounding sidewalks or patio levels.

Spend more time rolling a sandy soil and less time rolling a clay soil. With clay soil, never overdo the rolling.

## SEEDING A NEW LAWN

You can find plenty of advice on how to seed a new lawn. Here's the way I do it—and it works well for me.

After the soil has been fertilized and you've adjusted the pH with lime or soil sulfur; added gypsum for clay soils; added manure or other organic matter for extra humus; and tilled up, then rolled smooth, the whole thing, now you get to seed it. See chapter 2 to pick exactly the right kind of grass for your lawn. The worst mistake you could make would be to plant seed of a species that just won't thrive where you live.

Each type of grass seed will come with different recommendations as to how many pounds should be used per thousand square feet of lawn. This can run as low as two pounds of hybrid Bermuda grass seed per thousand to as high as twenty pounds of perennial ryegrass seed per thousand square feet. Actually, I've seen golf course greens overseeded with as much as forty pounds of perennial ryegrass seed. Check appendix A for recommended seeding rates for each type of grass.

Sometimes the printed advice on prepackaged grass seed tends to exaggerate how much square footage can be covered with seed. It's usually safer to use a little bit more than advised on the box. Never use less.

The grass seed is best spread using a drop spreader, which you can rent or borrow from the nursery where you shop. If you instead use a whirlybird-type spreader, cut the rate in half and first seed from one direction, then repeat from the other direction. If you insist on spreading your grass seed by hand, it's generally done with a side-to-side underhand motion. Try not to get too much seed in any one spot.

For seed mulch, I combine one part composted chicken manure with five parts steer manure. Mix this with a shovel in a wheelbarrow or in a large, empty trash can. You can spread this mix with a manure spreader (another tool to borrow from the nursery) or use the underhand method to sprinkle it on by hand. I've also had good luck just tossing the manure with a shovel.

You'll get good and dirty doing this, but hey, it's only manure, right?

I try to cover all the seed with between a quarter inch and half an inch of mulch. Look over the whole job when you think you're done—you'll probably find a few more spots to add a little more. Any seed not covered will either dry out or be eaten by sparrows. If there are a few spots where the mulch got on too thick, go over these very lightly with a garden rake.

Some gardeners like to add straw after they've put down the mulch, essentially to keep the surface from drying out while the grass seed is germinating. I don't use straw for starting seeded lawns, but if you want to, make sure it's straw and not hay that you're using. Hay will have too many weed seeds. A typical "square bale" of straw—which of course isn't square, but rather rectangular in shape—will cover around two thousand square feet of seeded soil. Don't add the straw too thickly or you'll never see your new lawn.

Until the new grass is up and actively growing, you'll need to keep the seedbed uniformly moist. There's no reason at this point to water deeply. What you're trying to do is keep the top inch or so of soil moist. If the weather is at all hot, you may have to sprinkle three or four times every day until your lawn is up and growing.

Another interesting way to start new grass seed is to sprinkle on the seed and fertilizer and then, instead of using straw or manure, just cover the whole thing with a big piece of polyester landscape fabric. One of the very best of these products is the Reemay Lawn & Garden Blanket. These lawn blankets are inexpensive, reusable, lightweight, strong, and easy to use. Sunlight will pass right through the blanket, and you can water the new seed or plants right through it, too. The blanket can be secured at the edges with pegs or simply by placing rocks on it to hold it down. The lawn blankets do a very good job of protecting the new seed from marauding birds, especially those seed-stealing sparrows.

The only real drawback to just covering seed with a lawn blanket is that it adds no fertility to the mix, nor does it provide anything new for the seed to sprout in. With this in mind, when I recently seeded a new patch of lawn I put down the seed and fertilizer, then just barely covered the seed with manure—an eighth of an inch or less. Then I put the lawn blanket over it all and watered through the blanket. I found that the soil under the blanket dried up more slowly than normal, so I didn't need to sprinkle the new seed as often. The new grass seed sprouted quickly and uniformly. I was impressed with the product.

Try to keep off the newly seeded lawn as much as possible for the first three weeks. Pound some sticks in the ground around the corners of the new lawn and run strings around the whole thing. Tie a few small flags of plastic or cloth on the string. These are your markers, telling people, in effect, *Keep off the lawn!*

If you see some weeds popping up here and there in the new grass after a few weeks, you might want to get into it to do a little hand-weeding. Place long, flat boards on the lawn and walk only on these. Don't use any herbicides on new grass.

As the grass starts actively growing, cut the irrigations back to twice a day, and then after a week or so to once a day. Increase the length of time that you irrigate, because now you're trying to encourage deep rooting of the grass.

When the grass is at least three inches tall, you can mow it for the first time. Do not mow the grass if the soil is still damp. Let it dry out a bit first. Don't remove more than one inch of grass with this first mowing, and use a catcher on your mower for the first few mowings. With newly started grass, the first few mowings in particular will produce grass clippings that are full of moisture. These clippings can smother the new seedlings below, robbing them of needed sunlight. This is why I always remove the grass clippings from newly planted lawns.

Each time you mow this new lawn, it will look better and better as the new grasses fill in and mature. A few months after seeding, your new lawn ought to be looking prime.

CHAPTER 9

# Animals, Wanted and Unwanted

We can't discuss problem lawns without discussing animals—both the kind we share our yards with willingly and the ones that show up uninvited.

## Pets

The pet problem I hear about most is the damage that dogs do to lawns by peeing on them. If you can train your dog to use one corner of the yard for his business, this is the best approach. Ideally, the dog will have his own small area with some dirt and lawn. It's helpful to set off this part of the yard with string and stakes, giving the dog a visual idea of what's off limits. I know several people who've trained their dogs in this way; every few months, they buy a few yards of cheap sod and replace the old damaged sod in the dog's area. Over the course of a year this isn't very expensive, and it keeps the rest of the lawn looking great.

It's also important to leave the dog a small area with some dirt to dig in. Many dogs like to dig, and they can be taught to dig in one area.

Spots of grass ruined from dog urine should be dug out and reseeded; you can also replace the grass with some matching sod. See chapter 8.

The best thing to do with dog poop is clean it up quickly with a shovel. This should be done every single day if needed. The longer it sits on the lawn, the more damage it will do. If the dog poop is soft and some of it sticks to the lawn after you've removed it, wash down the spot with a hose. If this is a constant problem, consider making changes in the dog's diet.

All dogs need daily exercise. A long walk every day will burn up excess energy and usually results in a dog that's less likely to tear up your lawn. The walk is good exercise for you, too!

## POISONOUS PLANTS

If you have pet cats in your yard, be aware that the ground cover wandering Jew can cause allergic reactions in them. It's best not to use this with cats around. Pets will occasionally chew on some of your landscape plants, some of which can be quite poisonous. If you have pets, avoid the following poisonous landscape plants:

- Arnica
- Azalea
- Bleeding hearts
- Buckeye
- Castor-oil plant
- Euphorbia
- Foxglove
- Hydrangea
- Monkshood
- Oleander
- Pencil tree
- Rosary pea
- Rue
- Sneezeweed
- Yellow oleander
- Yew

In addition, while heavenly bamboo *(Nandina domestica)* isn't poisonous for most animals, it is for dogs. Likewise, onions and onion-related plants are especially toxic to cats, as is spider plant. If mushrooms sprout in your lawn, pull them up and get rid of them. Don't leave them where the dog might get into them. If you keep getting mushrooms in the lawn you may be overwatering, or your drainage may need to be improved, or both! If you're interested in allergies that our pets get and how to avoid them, and want to see a very large listing of poisonous landscape plants, have a look at my book *Safe Sex in the Garden*.

### ALLERGIES

Dogs and cats can and do get allergies, and they can also be affected by pollen from our landscape plants. Plants that would cause us pollen allergies may do the same to our pets. Avoid using male landscape trees and shrubs in your yard if you want to limit the allergenic pollen. Both you and your pets will be better off without these male plants. For a complete listing of pollen-free plants, see my book *Allergy-Free Gardening*.

### SLUG AND SNAIL BAIT

Many dogs have been poisoned and killed after they got into a box of slug and snail bait. Switch over to the new kind of snail bait, the one with iron phosphate as its main ingredient (Sluggo). This product kills snails and slugs very effectively but is safe for pets. As a bonus, the iron phosphate breaks down in the garden and will actually provide some fertilizer.

### INSECTICIDES, HERBICIDES, AND FUNGICIDES

Everything you put on your lawn will affect the dogs and cats that play there. All the chemicals that are used for killing weeds, insects, or fungi are potentially dangerous to your pets. Keep pets off any newly treated lawn! Consider having a more managed lawn in your front yard, with an organic lawn in back where your pets are. See chapter 11 on organic lawns for tips on manures and other nonchemical products.

# Gophers

A few gophers can tear up a nice lawn in short order. Even if you're a complete animal lover, you don't want gophers in your yard. After they destroy your lawn, they'll start eating the roots and killing your roses, fruit trees, any attempt at a vegetable garden, the bulbs you plant, and so forth. Gophers and gardening don't go together at all! The gophers have got to go.

I have had many run-ins with gophers in my years of gardening, and I've always been successful in getting them out of the lawn and garden. I don't like killing them—or any animals, for that matter—but gophers usually don't give you much choice.

A lot of the following gopher-eradication information overlaps with mole-control material, as you'll see. Moles are also annoying enough to have their own section later in this chapter.

## POISONS

Resist the urge to use gopher or mole poisons. These poisons only work so-so, and the poisoned rodents can easily be eaten by predators such as owls, snakes, cats, or foxes—and then they'll die, too. If the predators are killed off, the rodent population, unchecked, will quickly explode in number.

## BARN OWLS

If you're out in the country, one of the best ways to get rid of both gophers and moles is to put up nesting boxes for barn owls. These big nesting boxes are generally perched on the top of eleven- to twenty-foot-tall poles. Place the boxes and their poles away from the house (forty feet or more if possible), but not too far from the lawns and yards. A nesting family of barn owls will eat thousands of rodents each season, and they're very good at catching gophers and moles. If you live in an area where palm trees grow, and you don't trim off the dead branches that accumulate below the crown, sooner or later a barn owl will move in and set up home. Take advantage of this and leave a palm tree unsheared. The number of rats, mice, moles, ground squirrels, and gophers that one owl can kill and eat is quite incredible. Many orchards and vineyards now sport owl boxes, one for every three or four acres. The owls are saving the farmers a lot of money.

Nesting boxes for barn owls are usually made from plywood; the roof is slanted so water will run off. Sometimes the roof is shingled, too. A nesting box for barn owls should be a minimum of twelve by twelve inches for the floor, and at least sixteen inches deep. Place small drain holes in the corners of the floor, and drill small holes around the top of the box on each side for air circulation. It's best to design the box so that it can be cleaned out easily once a year when the owls are gone.

The box should have only one opening, and this must be at least three and a half inches in diameter but no more than five inches wide. Too large an entrance hole will let great horned owls in, and they'll eat up the barn owls. Horned owls eat rodents, too, but they aren't nearly as tough on rodents as the smaller barn owls. Horned owls may also eat your cats and small dogs!

If you'd like to buy good barn owl boxes already made (they'll ship them to you), see the Owl Nestbox Resource Page listed in the Resources section of this book. At this site, you can also find more detailed instructions on building your own owl boxes. The bottom line with barn owls is that they're the most effective rodent killers in existence.

The right family cat can also be a pretty good rodent catcher.

## GOPHER SNAKES!

I also know of quite a few people who've caught gopher snakes and then released them on their own property. The best way to catch a gopher snake or two is to drive very slowly in the country on a paved road that gets little traffic. Pin the snake's head down with a stick, pick it up firmly from behind the head, and stick it in an old pillowcase. Gopher snakes aren't poisonous but they will often bite, and the bites don't feel good. The best time to go looking for gopher snakes is in spring and early summer, just before and just after dark. Evenings that are cold and windy will produce no snakes; nights with full moons are likewise not productive. Gopher snakes are, like barn owls, designed by nature to catch and eat gophers and moles.

### GOPHER TRAPS

There are a number of gopher traps on the market, but by far the best is the old Macabee gopher trap made of heavy wire. These are tricky to set if you've never done it before, so buy them at a farm supply store and ask someone there to show you exactly how it's done before you leave the store.

Trapping gophers is very effective if done right. Start by tying a wire about two feet long onto the end of the gopher trap and securing it to a sturdy metal or wooden stake. Now find the newest, freshest gopher mound, dig out its opening with a shovel, open up the tunnel, and place the trap as far into the hole as possible.

Next, pound the stake down near the hole but not into the tunnel itself. The stake and wire will ensure that you don't lose the trap. A trapped gopher may easily draw the attention of a cat, dog, hawk, owl, skunk, or fox, which will try to run off with your gopher and your trap. The wire and stake keep that from happening.

Leave the opening of the hole open. The light coming into the hole will serve as bait, since the gophers intended for that hole to be closed.

Set several traps in different holes if possible. Check the traps at least once a day and reset them if you've killed a gopher or if the gopher has set off the trap and gotten away.

One last word about trapping gophers: Macabee gopher traps often just catch a gopher and don't kill it. You have to do that yourself. Not fun. There are traps made for catching gophers alive, so that you can then release them somewhere else (in the yard of someone you're not too fond of?). The problem with these live traps, however, is that they don't work very well.

### WATER, SMOKE BOMBS, AND ROAD FLARES

Sometimes you can get gophers—moles, too—to move out of your territory just by flooding their holes. By all means go ahead and stick the garden hose down a few holes and give this a try. Usually, though, this doesn't work very well, if at all.

Smoking them out is much more effective. Special gopher smoker bombs are sold in all good nurseries, and these work pretty well. Even better are regular red road flares, which you can buy very cheaply at an auto parts store. They usually come in several lengths; the longer ones burn longer and are more effective. Still, road flares of any length work pretty well.

Dig out the gopher mound and open up the tunnel. Light the road flare by twisting off the cap and then striking the tip of the flare with the end of the cap. Point it away from yourself so you don't get burned.

Shove the lit end of the road flare into the gopher tunnel and then shovel some dirt back over the top of the opening. Stamp it all shut tight with the sole of your shoe. You'll see some of the smoke escaping up through the dirt. If you spot smoke coming up from another hole in the lawn, quickly go over there and plug it up.

The smoke from road flares is sulfurous and it'll stink out the entire tunnel. On occasion, the gophers will be asphyxiated from the smoke and die in the tunnels. More often, though, they will take off for anywhere far away from that stinky sulfur smoke. The smoke and its smell will persist in the tunnel for some time, and the gophers will often simply abandon the tunnel.

The gophers may well make several more attacks on your lawn and flower beds, and you may need to smoke them several times and in several different tunnels to get rid of them for good. If the smoking doesn't work for you, buy some gopher traps . . . or get a gopher snake.

## Moles

Moles are much smaller than gophers, and their tunnels often run just under the surface of a lawn. Often you can just look at your yard and see exactly where mole tunnels are—they're pushed up just under the surface.

Moles are insect eaters and they don't actually eat any of your lawn at all. They seem to be much more common in high-rainfall areas and are rare in drier, irrigated-lawn areas.

### MOLES AND GRUBS

There are many different traps made for killing moles, but resist the urge to buy and use these. Poison baits for moles are not a good idea, either. Moles are tunneling through your lawn for a reason. If you have moles, rest assured that you have a lot of grubs in the lawn, too. The moles are eating these grubs, which are up to about an inch long, are usually white or gray, and often have brown heads. Areas where grub infestations are especially thick are often marked by patches of dying grass.

> ***Insider's Tip***
>
> If you have a dead patch of lawn whose center is totally dead, but the edges are extra green, this damage isn't from grubs, it's from dog urine. The nitrogen in the urine fertilizes whatever grass it doesn't outright kill. This is why the edges of the patch will be greener than the rest of the lawn.

Sometimes a grub-infested lawn will attract nighttime raids by skunks. The skunks (and occasionally raccoons, too) will tear up pieces of your lawn as they dig up grubs to eat. The solution here is much the same as it is for getting rid of the moles: Kill the grubs. These grubs are larvae from any number of insect pests. Left unchecked, they may well destroy most of your lawn by themselves—not to mention all the damage done by the critters they attract.

There are a number of organic and inorganic methods of killing off lawn grubs. Flooding the lawn seems to help to bring the grubs up closer to the surface, where they'll be easier to kill with biocontrols. Look for sources of these biocontrols in the Resources section of this book, under integrated pest management (IPM).

Most soil grubs are larvae of some kind of beetle. Japanese beetle larvae can be attacked with milky spore, an organic product that only attacks Japanese beetles. *Heterorhabditis bacteriophora* nematodes have shown good results for white grub control. Nematodes are tiny soil wireworms. This particular species will find the white grubs and kill them. These beneficial nematodes are available in mail-order catalogs, often sold as Hb nematodes. They should be applied to already thoroughly watered lawns late in the day and then watered in immediately. They won't damage the lawn or other garden plants. They work fastest in sandy soils and slower in heavy, clay soils.

Organic insecticides can also be used as a drench on your lawns; sometimes they're quite effective. A mix of water, soap, pyrethrum, and rotenone will often kill most of the grubs—although even organic insecticides will also kill off earthworms and other beneficial soil organisms.

### CHEMICAL GRUB CONTROL

For a chemical approach to soil grubs, a single treatment can be made between mid-July and mid-August. Commonly used chemical insecticides are chlorpyrifos (Dursban), carbaryl (Sevin), and soil diazinon. The pesticide must be watered into the soil well after use, or it won't be effective.

Keep in mind that no chemical insecticide is healthful for the family dog, cat, the kids, or the songbirds that might well eat some of the chemically poisoned earthworms or grubs.

Some lawn experts recommend use of the chemicals trichlorfon (Dylox), imidacloprid (Merit), or halofenozide (GrubEx) in midsummer as a preventive measure against lawn grubs.

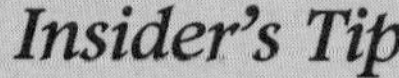

## Insider's Tip

Information about different horticultural chemicals can quickly become out of date. When these chemicals are in use for any period of time, they often become associated with various health hazards and are banned. In some cases, certain chemicals can only be purchased by farmers or licensed contractors. For these reasons, you won't find a great deal of specific chemical recommendations in this book. Old chemicals are constantly being removed from the market, and new ones are introduced all the time. Sometimes the only sensible thing to do is to go to a good nursery, look over all the new products, and then decide what you want to use.

### OTHER PREVENTIVE MEASURES

- Keeping a lawn healthy won't keep grubs and moles out of it, but a healthy lawn can recuperate much faster after an attack.
- Mowing the lawn too short will weaken it and leave it more easily damaged by grubs. Mowing higher promotes a stronger root system. There is evidence, too, that grubs, like most insect pests, prefer unhealthy lawns to healthy ones.
- Keeping the nitrogen levels up and maintaining a good amount of humus in the soil sometimes helps lessen the chance of grub damage. Grubs will attack any species of lawn, although the worst damage is usually seen on bluegrass lawns.
- Aerating the lawn makes for stronger roots and also gives birds a better shot at picking out grubs. Many birds that are attracted to birdfeeders and suet feeders will also eat both the grubs and the beetles that the grubs come from. Encourage wild birds in your yard.

- When you water, water deeply. This will also help develop a stronger root system.
- Overseed bluegrass lawns each spring with a mix of fescue or perennial ryegrass seed. If the grubs ruin the bluegrass, you'll still have a lawn.
- In heavily grub-damaged lawns, take a rake and rake up the exposed soil; this will expose the grubs to the birds.
- Soak grub-infested areas with soapy water. Use a quart of liquid dish soap to several gallons of water and soak the lawn with this mix. It will kill grubs.
- Sometimes grubs can be held in check by dusting the lawn several times with diatomaceous earth. This safe product kills grubs that come to the surface to eat grass blades.
- Lastly, some people don spiked strap-on sandals and walk around their lawns, spearing grubs as they go. Of course, they're aerating the lawn at the same time. I have no idea how effective this method is, but hey, it can't hurt.

# PART FOUR
# Special Considerations

CHAPTER 10

# Really Large Lawns

## Farm Tractors

If you have acres of lawn to mow, consider buying a real farm tractor instead of a riding lawn mower. New, real tractors are very expensive, but sometimes a used one can be an incredible bargain. If you've never driven a tractor before, don't worry. Usually you can be shown how to operate it in a matter of minutes—they're easy to drive.

In recent years, there has been an unfortunate trend toward bigger and bigger farms. As a result, there are many farm auctions where smaller farms are selling out. The giant farmers have no use for these small tractors, so the prices are often downright cheap.

Most farm tractors are extra solid. They are built to run for hundreds of thousands of hours. Even a tractor that is well over fifty years old may still be perfectly good. There are a ton of old Ford tractors, 8Ns and 9Ns, around; these go way back but are still terrific small tractors. You'll often find these old Fords painted in the original colors, red and gray. Most of the used tractors you'll be interested in will have somewhere between twenty and fifty horsepower.

More really good old tractors to look out for are old Allis-Chalmers B and C models, as well as some of the old International Farmall tractors. The Allis-Chalmers are usually painted orange, while the old Internationals are usually fire-engine red. These are all early-1950s tractors, but if they were kept up at all, they can be terrific buys.

## *Insider's Tip*

John Deere makes some of the very finest tractors of all. They're usually painted farm green. John Deere tractors were once all built in the United States and were built to last, and there are a lot of old ones around. If you can find a small older John Deere in decent shape that doesn't have a narrow front end, it might be one to consider. In recent years, however, some of the smaller John Deere tractors have been built outside the U.S. This is especially true of some of the company's lawn mowers and edgers. The quality of these foreign-built John Deere tractors and mowers is not as good. My advice: Don't buy them.

### TRACTOR SAFETY

Tractors are very dangerous on steep slopes, and many farmers get killed when they roll their tractors, often while trying to mow the weeds in a ditch. If your property is steep, don't buy a tractor. But if your property and lawn are large and fairly level, do consider it. Tractors can be quite safe if you keep a few things in mind.

- **Don't buy a narrow-front tractor.** These are the models that have the two front wheels right next to each other. Such tractors do have their uses, but they're dangerous. The narrow front can easily fall down into a hole or get stuck in the mud. The steering wheel can sometimes spin out of control if the front wheels get jammed. You can break a thumb on these. The narrow-front tractors are much more prone to tipping over, too. Don't buy one! Get a wide-front tractor instead.
- **Don't drive a tractor on steep ground.** As mentioned earlier, tractors of all types are prone to tip over on their sides on steep slopes. Also, do not drive down into ditches—and don't drive up steep slopes, either. All can result in a deadly rollover.

- **PTO.** This stands for "power takeoff." The PTO is a shaft that sticks out usually from the back of the tractor. It spins when you engage it (usually with a lever); it's what supplies the power to drive power equipment such as mowers and hay balers. The PTO shaft is probably the most dangerous part of a tractor! It should be covered with a safety shield, but these are often missing on older models. Still, even if the PTO has a cover on it, always treat it with the utmost respect. When I farmed, I saw all too many farmers who'd had accidents involving PTO shafts. The moving shaft can catch a wayward shirtsleeve or loose pant leg, and the results can be deadly. I always treat any moving PTO shaft the same way I do a loaded gun: with plenty of respect. Never wear loose clothes while running a PTO. There's a reason farmers like those tight-fitting Lee jeans. Nonetheless, if you always take precautions, a PTO is a darn useful tool.

- **Never drive a tractor fast.** Most tractors have what is called highway gear—a very high gear. While in the highway gear, the tractor will go much faster than normal, and this is exceedingly dangerous. My advice: Don't drive on the highway at all, and never use your highway gear. Tractors just are not built for speed, and running them too fast is asking for trouble.

- **Don't let people ride on the fenders.** This is tempting—and in fact it's done all the time—but it's a bad idea. Only one person at a time should be on the tractor. I once attended a very sad funeral for a farm kid who'd fallen off the fender and was then run over by the rear wheels.

- **Don't let kids drive the tractor.** Tractors are very simple to run, and they're fun besides. Kids will always want to drive them. I suggest you don't let them do so. Kids and tractors can be a deadly mix. Keep the key to the tractor in your pocket. Don't leave it in the ignition; it will only tempt the kids when you're not there.

- **Get a tractor that has a battery and a working electrical starter.** Many older models also have a hand crank on the front, to use when the battery or starter motor won't work. Each sort of tractor is different to crank—some easy, some difficult. Keep in mind, however, that while you're cranking on the tractor engine, it can backfire and the crank can go crazy in your hands. I once knocked myself out cold while trying to hand-crank an old Allis-Chalmers WD tractor. I was just lucky I didn't lose all my teeth! Keep the battery charged up; if the starter goes bad, buy a rebuilt one and put it on.

- **Turn it off.** Whenever you're working on or adjusting any power attachments to the tractor, such as a mower, turn off the engine first. Do not trust in simply putting the transmission in neutral and turning off the PTO. Actually shut down the tractor first and you'll be much safer. Power equipment run by a tractor PTO has much more power than ordinary equipment. This equipment is extremely useful and efficient but is always potentially dangerous if supplied with power. Shut it down first!

## HOW TO BUY A USED FARM TRACTOR

The very best place to get a killer deal on a small used farm tractor is at a farm auction.

- Before you go to the auction, take a look at used farm equipment dealers and see what kind of money they're asking for different models. This will give you a good idea of what is a good buy, and what isn't.
- Farm auctioneers almost always print out flyers several weeks beforehand listing what will be for sale. You can contact auctioneers by phone and ask to be sent flyers. This way you can avoid going to auctions that don't have what you want.
- The very best deals of all are to be had on weekday auctions. The worst deals are on Saturday auctions.
- Generally, the smaller the crowd, the better the deals.
- You can quickly spend more money than you intended to at a farm auction! Have an idea of your top price firmly in mind

before you make the first bid. If the bidding goes past that number, bail out. An auction is no place to act competitively, but people do it all the time.

- If you see a tractor that you're interested in, ask one of the people in charge to start it up for you. Pay close attention to how easy it is to start, and how well it runs. See if it smokes. If the tractor won't start and idle smoothly, forget it. You don't want it.

- Take a look at the tires. Really old tractors didn't even have rubber tires; they had steel tires. You don't need one of those! See how worn the tires are, and if there are any rips in the sides. Tractor tires are very expensive, so if it has good ones, that's a big plus.

- Don't start the bidding for an item you want. Let someone else open. Don't be in a hurry to raise the first bid; take your time.

- Never raise bids by more than ten or twenty dollars at a time.

- Act as if you really don't care all that much whether you end up buying the tractor. If it seems like you just have to have it, this only encourages other people to bid aggressively against you.

- Don't come to a farm auction wearing fancy clothes. Blend in. If you look like you have a lot of money to blow, other people will keep raising the bids on you.

- When you get to the auction, look around and see if there is a small tractor that you'd like to own. If there is, go and register with the bank. Generally these auctions include a representative of a bank; in order to make bids, you need to register and get a number. It costs you nothing to register.

- Walk around and talk to the bank people or the owner and see if there is someone there who will haul the tractor from the auction to your place for you. At almost all farm auctions, you'll find a number of fellows with heavy trucks and trailers who will haul the tractor for you for a price—often quite a reasonable one. If there's no one there to haul, ask the banker before you bid whether you could leave a tractor on site until you can have it moved.

- The very best deals to be had on old tractors are deep in farm country, not close to any city. Near cities, there will be city folks bidding up the prices. It may cost you more to have the tractor hauled a greater distance, but you'll usually still save money by going to auctions farther away from town.
- Remember, at an auction all sales are final! If you make the top bid on something, you just bought it. There's no backing down.

### *Insider's Tip*

Never buy a used farm tractor from a junk dealer or wrecking yard. These folks know dozens of ways to make a complete junker seem like a good deal. I used to live on a farm in Minnesota right off Highway 210. Up the road a ways was a junkyard that often sold "rebuilt" tractors with fresh coats of paint to unwary passersby. They had many clever ways to hide a cracked engine block. But once the tractor was sold, the only guarantee it ever had was "the 210 Guarantee": Once it hit Highway 210, that was the end of the guarantee.

## EQUIPMENT TO GO WITH THE TRACTOR

If you buy a tractor, you'll also need some equipment. Once in a while the equipment will be sold with the tractor, but not usually.

- **Sickle bar mowers.** These are what the old-timers used to mow their hay. Today sickle bar mowers mostly are used for mowing down tall weeds. They run off power from the tractor's PTO. You wouldn't want to mow lawns with sickle bar mowers but for cutting down really tall grass and weeds, they're pretty effective. The bar is usually about five to seven feet long and cuts with a scissor-type action. If you buy a sickle bar mower, treat it with respect. It wouldn't be too hard to cut off a finger with this kind of mower. Used, old, but still decent sickle bar mowers can often be bought at auctions for between one and four hundred dollars.

- **Gang mowers, tow mowers, and drag-behind nonmotorized reel-type turn mowers.** These mowers—often several of them are linked together to cover more lawn area—are dragged behind the tractor and mow much the same way a simple reel push mower does. These work very well and do a superior job of cutting grass, provided that the lawn is fairly level and weed-free. Gang mowers are popular with golf courses. With a small gang of three reel mowers pulled by a twenty-horsepower tractor, you can mow several acres of grass in an hour. Clippings are not collected but are well distributed. I have seen a gang of these mowers that would cut an eight-foot-wide swath of grass sold new for around twelve hundred dollars. I do think it's a good idea to buy these mowers new. To find a source, just do a simple Internet search using the term "gang mowers."
- **Pull-behind rotary mowers.** These run off the power supplied by the tractor's PTO shaft. They're very good for mowing large areas of lawn, especially if the lawns are weedy and less than perfect. They do a fairly nice job of lawn mowing, but not nearly as nice as the results from pulling a gang of reel mowers.
- **Brush hogs.** A brush hog is a large, pull-behind-the-tractor type of rotary lawn mower, often with several blades. Brush hogs are heavy, strong, and will mow down brush and the toughest weeds. You could use one now and then to mow a lawn that has gotten out of control and far too tall. Just don't expect it to do a very nice job of lawn mowing.
- **Other tractor attachments.** At auctions, you can often find very good deals on tractor-run equipment such as front-end

loaders, posthole augers, power sprayers, snowblowers, and so on. Some of the equipment, including power sprayers, snowblowers, and power augers, will run on power from the PTO. Front-end loaders are powered by the tractor's hydraulic system. Occasionally, you'll see someone using a tractor PTO to run a large saw blade for cutting firewood. This is a very risky proposition and not one I'd recommend. I have also seen PTO-driven log splitters and wasn't impressed with them, either.

## TRACTOR MAINTENANCE

- Many tractors sit out in the rain and snow, but they last longer and work better if they can at least be parked under some sort of a lean-to or pole barn.
- Tractors, just like cars, need oil in their engines. Always check the oil before using one. In cold weather, use ten-weight oil. In summer, use thirty- or forty-weight oil. Never run a tractor low on oil.
- Change the oil and oil filter on your tractor several times a year. It's a good idea to pencil in this task on your calendar ahead of time. Change the oil three times a year if you run it in winter.
- Keep the tractor tires aired up properly and they will last much longer.
- Almost all tractors have water-cooled radiators. Check the fluid level in the radiator at regular intervals. Most older models don't have temperature gauges, and even if they do, the gauges aren't entirely reliable. Make sure you add antifreeze to the water in the radiator. By the way, keep in mind that many kinds of antifreeze are attractive to large animals and are also quite poisonous.
- Keep the posts on the tractor battery clean and corrosion-free at all times.
- When you change your oil, it's a good time to go over the tractor and check all belts. Replace any that are worn or cracked.

- An older tractor will have zerk fittings, spots where you can add lube to stop friction. If you don't know what a zerk fitting is, have anyone with tractor or automobile repair experience show you. You'll need to buy yourself some tubes of lube and a simple, inexpensive lube gun. I suggest you locate every single zerk fitting on your tractor. Count them and write down the number. Each time you lube the tractor, count the ones you've done, and make sure you get to all of them. Much of the power equipment you buy will also have zerk fittings. The more often you lube your tractor and your machinery, the longer it will last.

## Hiring a Professional

Another approach to large or complex lawns is hiring a professional to do it for you. The first thing to note is that there's a difference between a lawn care person and an all-around gardener.

### LAWN CARE PROFESSIONALS

Lawn specialists should be able to tell you what sort of a program they'd put your lawn on, and what you ought to be able to expect from hiring them. Any schedule they might work up for your lawn would need to include planned, regular fertilization and some plan for keeping weeds down. Don't be afraid to ask for before-and-after photos of some of their lawns.

Lawn care people will do all the mowing, edging, and lawn upkeep. The costs for these services for a lawn of between three and four thousand square feet could run anywhere from a low of forty dollars a month to a high of around three hundred. Expect to pay more for larger lawns. If the offered price sounds high to you, by all means shop around before you sign any agreements.

### Potential Pitfall

Any agreement you sign with a landscaping professional should include a clause that lets you terminate the arrangement anytime you are not pleased with the services. Do not sign any agreement with any lawn care company that doesn't include this escape clause.

One of the better ways to find a good lawn care company is to ask neighbors who use one if they're pleased with it. Or you could go to a nursery where professional landscapers shop and ask whom the folks there would recommend. There are also almost always ads for lawn care people in the classifieds of every local newspaper. Ask anyone you hire for several phone numbers of happy customers whom you might call as recommendations.

If you have read and understood this book, you can probably make your own lawn decisions perfectly well. In this case, you might simply want to hire someone to mow and edge your lawns weekly, as well as doing other lawn tasks as needed. You will find that a great many so-called gardeners know very little about gardening and are mostly just experienced at mowing lawns.

## HIRING GARDENERS

If you can afford a terrific gardener, then do consider hiring one. The best gardeners can do it all—lawns, trees, shrubs, annuals, perennials, you name it. They love to garden, know a great deal about it, are flexible, work fast, and do things right. A good gardener can and will give you plenty of advice, but will also keep in mind that it's your yard, and you are the boss.

## *Insider's Tip*

One of the oldest tricks in the book to see how good gardeners are involves asking them about several plants that are common to your area—using their scientific names. Latin names are the language that serious gardeners use often, and if prospective gardeners can't sling some of these around comfortably, then they're automatically suspect. I taught landscape gardening for many years and always told my students, "The difference between a gardener who can use and understand Latin names, and one who can't, is about twenty bucks an hour."

A good gardener always cleans up afterward and never leaves tools lying around when the work is done. I would seriously consider getting rid of any gardener who did.

The price that is paid per hour for gardeners varies widely from one area to another and is very difficult to pin down. Typical hourly rates are between ten and twenty dollars, yet I know many who charge and get more than double that. Some of the very best gardeners, once they are established in an area, can charge almost whatever they want and still have plenty of work.

If you're ever lucky enough to find very experienced, very good gardeners who are easy to get along with and keep your lawns and yards looking great, hang on to them. By the way, many more women are now doing gardening work professionally than in the past, and from what I've seen most of them make darn good gardeners, too.

## *Potential Pitfall*

With certain jobs, such as installing a new lawn or dethatching an old one, always ask for a written estimate of the costs ahead of time.

CHAPTER 11

# An Organic Approach to Lawns

It isn't my aim in this book to push or promote either organic or chemical methods of lawn care. I feel that my readers are perfectly intelligent people; my job is to present both sides as fairly as possible, and let you decide for yourself.

That said, there's no particular reason why you can't borrow from each point of view, using some of each. You can be just as pure as you like.

I belong to the largest group of people who write about gardening, the Garden Writers Association (GWA). I get e-mail from other members daily on one subject or another. One theme that pops up almost every day is organics. The majority of today's garden writers are firmly in favor of using organic methods as opposed to chemical. Let's explore some of the best ways to maintain a quality lawn organically.

## Manure

The main organic fertilizer used on lawns is steer manure, which has low amounts of NPK—nitrogen, phosphorus, and potassium. It also contains many important micronutrients that are crucial to lawn growth.

### STEER MANURE VERSUS COW MANURE

Generally, manure sold as "steer manure" is collected from feedlots. As such, these cattle are fed on hay and grain and not on pasture. Because of this, this manure will not contain many weed seeds. Manure sold as "cow manure" may well be from dairies where the cows are pastured, and are eating weeds. Cattle chomp down forage, and in the process a great many weed seeds will pass right through a cow's system unharmed. If you spread manure on your lawn that's full of weed seeds, you're going to soon have a lawn full of weeds. Buy manure labeled "steer manure" and save yourself this problem.

### HORSE MANURE

Sometimes you can get all the horse manure you want for free as long as you're willing to go and shovel it yourself. You may well be told that it is great manure and that it's perfectly safe to spread on your lawn. Don't believe this!

Horse manure that is at all fresh is very high in salt, and salt will burn your lawn. Likewise, using fresh horse manure as mulch around your other landscape plants may well kill them. Fresh horse manure will also usually contain a huge amount of weed seeds.

Well-aged horse manure—horse manure that has been composted for several years—is actually a great organic fertilizer product, but it's hard to find. If you have a ton of land, you might want to consider getting a large pile of fresh horse manure (if it's free) and then composting it for several years before you use it. Let me caution you about this, though: Any large batch of fresh horse manure will almost always contain millions of fly eggs and larvae. If you don't mind hordes of houseflies and horseflies, by all means go for it. My advice, though: Pass on the free horse manure. It probably isn't worth the trouble.

### SHEEP AND GOAT MANURE

Manure from goats and sheep comes in little round pellets that, if spread on your lawn fresh, will bring unpleasant results. This same manure is richer than horse manure, however, and if you want to compost it first, then it might well be worth considering.

### HOG MANURE

Manure from pigs (or as their producers like to call 'em, swine) is very rich and contains few weed seeds, but you'd never want to use it fresh. Talk about stinky! Hog manure is about as smelly as manure can get. Hog manure that has been composted for a few years, though, is an excellent organic fertilizer, no longer smells bad, and is good stuff if you can find it.

### CHICKEN OR TURKEY MANURE

Fresh chicken manure can also often be had for free, if you're willing to go to the egg producer and shovel it yourself. Chicken manure is powerful stuff; if used fresh on a lawn, it'll burn the grass almost certainly. Fresh chicken manure also will generally contain millions of fly eggs and larvae. And this stuff smells incredibly bad!

There are, however, companies now that compost, bag, and sell chicken manure. Sometimes it's mixed with steer manure and sold as "composted blend." This is a terrific product and works especially well for establishing new lawns from seed. During the composting process, high heat is generated—usually enough to kill off all the weed seed and fly eggs and larvae.

### BAT GUANO

Bat guano is manure from bats, collected from huge bat caves, and it used to be fairly common and cheap. It is no longer either, and although it remains a high-quality organic fertilizer, it's too expensive to use on our lawns.

### RABBIT MANURE

Rabbit manure is richer than that of cow, steer, or horse, but not as rich as chicken manure. Rabbit manure is usually fairly free of weed seed but it, too, must be composted before using on a lawn. If you're so inclined and live near a rabbit producer, you can also sometimes get this fresh manure if you're willing to shovel it. It will bring with it plenty of flies, although not nearly so many as fresh chicken manure.

### ZOO DOO, OR MANURE FROM THE ZOO

In recent years, organic manure collected from zoos and then composted has become available. "Put the power of tigers and elephants to work in your yard!" was one of the more interesting claims I've seen for this product. No doubt composted zoo poo is a decent product, but again, it's far too expensive to use as lawn fertilizer. It might be fun to buy some, though, and put it under your roses. See what some rhino power will do?

## Applying Manure: Manure Spreaders

All the different kinds of manure mentioned above need to be spread with a manure spreader. Most of these are round wire drums with a handle. You dump the manure in the drum through a door, close it, and start spreading. The slower you pull, the more deeply the manure gets applied. These take a bit of getting used to, but they're actually pretty simple to use. They are not often seen for sale; generally, if you buy some manure the nursery will just lend you a spreader to use for the day. When you're done, you'll usually need to go over the whole lawn with a rake, spreading out the spots where you got the manure on too deep. Anything much over half an inch deep is probably too much for the average lawn.

## Other Kinds of Organic Supplements

### SOYBEAN MEAL

Soybean meal is generally thought of as a high-protein feed additive for dairy cattle and other farm animals, but it also makes a very decent organic fertilizer. Soybean meal is sold in fifty-pound sacks at feed stores, and compared to many other organic fertilizers it is low priced. Soybean meal, because it is already approved for animal feed, is usually low in chemical contaminants. It has around 7 percent slow-acting N (nitrogen) and small amounts of P (phosphorous) and K (potassium), plus numerous other micronutrients. Soybean meal is also ground fine, making it easy to apply to lawns, and it is a weed-free organic fertilizer. Often overlooked, soybean meal is a good-value material for organic lawns.

### COTTONSEED MEAL

Since cotton produces so many seeds, pulverized cottonseed has long been available as organic fertilizer. As fertilizer, cottonseed meal is moderately rich, slow releasing, and humus building. Still, it has some knocks against it. As a lawn fertilizer it's expensive; also, it isn't nearly as "organic" as you might think. Consider this: Of all the commercial farm crops, there is no other single crop that is treated with as many chemicals as cotton. These crops receive huge amounts of chemical fertilizers to grow, because they're well known for depleting soil nutrients. Cotton crops are frequently sprayed numerous times each season with various chemical fungicides, miticides, and insecticides. At the end of the season, they're often sprayed with herbicides to defoliate the plants for ease of cotton picking. All these chemicals find their way into the cottonseeds, making it a less-than-organic product—even if it does all come from seeds.

A last point here on cottonseed meal: If you are the slightest bit interested in organic gardening, don't use this material as fertilizer around your fruit trees, near vines, or in your vegetable garden. Those same cotton chemicals will end up in the fruit and vegetables you eat.

## Organic Methods of Weed Control

The surest method of organic lawn weed control is hand digging. For weeds that grow in cracks in the pavement, there are small burning units—mini-flamethrowers if you will—that can be used to burn the weeds away. Some gardeners claim they have good luck at killing weeds with a mix of vinegar and soap, but for me this mix seems to kill only the plants I like, not the ones I'm trying to get rid of.

Some people will spot-spray lawn weeds with a solution of Roundup, but even though Roundup (supposedly) biodegrades quickly, it isn't organic by any means. The surest way to a weed-free organic lawn would come from a combination of good, basic organic gardening practices. Here's a baker's dozen of them:

- Use organic manures on your lawn and use them often.
- Plant the right kind of grass in the first place—one well suited to your own particular microclimate.
- If any area is too wet, set up a decent system of drainage.
- If the soil is too acidic—below pH 5.5—then add some lime each year to raise the pH.
- If the soil is too alkaline—above pH 7.8—then add enough soil sulfur each year to bring it closer to neutral (7).
- Mow your lawns often, but don't mow them too low.
- Stay off lawns when they're wet or frozen.
- Rake tree leaves off your lawn if there are a lot of them. Compost these.
- Add some sifted compost as a topdressing to your lawn once or twice a year.
- Always overseed thin areas of the lawn.
- Keep your lawn well aerated.
- Pull weeds such as dandelions before they bloom and shed seeds all over the lawn.
- Anytime it's hot and dry, give your lawns a good, long, slow, deep soaking. Don't let them get too stressed for water.

The bottom line on weeds and lawns is that if kept healthy and happy, the right lawn grasses will almost always outgrow any kind of weed.

CHAPTER 12

# Ground Covers

"Give Up Your Lawn!" is advice I see all the time in garden magazines and on numerous Web sites. "Foolproof Ground Covers!"

"Ground Covers You Can Walk On!" is another headline you'll often find. "Ground covers take almost no water, no weeding, no fertilizer. They're no trouble- and labor-free!"

Well, if you believe all the above, I've got a bridge to sell you! First of all, if you spend much time walking on any ground cover except a lawn, it will look terrible. Really. Okay, some ground covers will take more foot traffic than others, and we'll explore that, but honestly, don't be fooled. Heavy foot traffic will quickly destroy almost any ground cover except a lawn.

How about the no-work, no-weeding, no-fertilizer, no-watering claims? I mean, come on! Who writes this stuff? Did they ever try to establish one of these foolproof ground covers?

People ask me all the time, "What's a ground cover that I can plant that won't take any work and will look good all the time?" I tell 'em, "Hey, good luck! There is no such ground cover, unless you mean a grass lawn."

The biggest problem with ground covers is weeds. If you leave ground bare, then weeds will grow in this open soil. Yes, you can put preemergent herbicides down, and they will slow the germination of weed seed. They will also slow the growth of the plants you're trying to get to cover the ground. Plan on doing plenty of hand-weeding unless you use plenty of mulch.

If for some reason you plant your ground cover plants and find yourself too busy to keep the new weeds under control, then what? Then you're in for some serious work! Getting weeds out of established ground covers is such a pain that it's often simpler to just rip the whole thing up and start over.

In Southern areas, common Bermuda grass seed is in all the soil. You can almost count on the fact that Bermuda will pop up in your new ground cover. If you let it take hold at all, you might be in for a real mess. A ground cover with Bermuda grass sticking up out of it looks remarkably trashy. And once the Bermuda is thriving in the ground cover, good luck at ever getting entirely rid of it.

Okay, so what about the low- or no-water claims? Well, in horticulture you often get what you pay for. You want plants that need almost no water at all? You can have them—xeriscaping is what they call this. But here's the real deal: Super-drought-tolerant plants hardly ever flower, and generally they're on the drab side. Oh, there are a few exceptions, but truthfully, *no water* usually translates to *not that great looking*. And anyhow, in order to get *any* ground cover established in the first place, you're going to have to keep it irrigated until it forms deep roots. And that might take a year or two.

So what about the fertilizer? Ground covers don't need fertilizer like lawns do, right? Well, maybe not as much, but again, in order to get that ground cover to grow in quickly and look good, unless your soil is super-rich, it will need fertilizer.

Okay, what's my point here? There's no such thing as a free lunch. Ground covers do have their place, and they can be darn handy, too—especially in shady spots where the grass just won't grow. But ground covers can be a ton of work, too, and if you plant the wrong kind for your area, you'll soon regret it.

I love visiting any nice nursery—I used to own one. But all too often in the nursery business, the number one thing is: They want to sell you stuff. If you suggest that your big lawn is too much trouble to mow and irrigate and keep up, and you're thinking of killing it all off and planting it into a pretty flowering ground cover of, say, blue star creeper, you'll probably be encouraged to go for it. Of course first they'll sell you Roundup to kill your lawn, then preemergent herbicide to kill the weed seed in the soil, then soil amendments, and starter fertilizer, and weed barriers, and flats and flats of ground cover, and some drip irrigation or maybe some micro-sprinklers, and of course lots of mulch.

Then a year later, if in all likelihood your ground cover still doesn't quite look like you had imagined, and you're disgusted with all the work and so little to show for it, what then? Well, then they can sell you more Roundup to kill off the plants that did grow, and some more fertilizer, more manure, and yep, some good grass seed (or sod) so you can get that nice old lawn back where it used to be. Sounds cynical, I suppose, but I've seen this exact thing happen, many times.

So what *is* the best ground cover of them all?

That's easy. The best ground cover there is for the money is a nice lawn. Heck, you can even walk on it! But sure, there are plenty of places where you might well want a ground cover that isn't grass. If you plant it right and pick the right kind for your particular area, a ground cover can work out okay.

## A Few Tips on Ground Covers

Before planting any ground cover, make sure you get the soil very weed-free. Planting your ground cover plants closer than recommended is a good idea, too, since they will fill in quicker and you'll have fewer weeds. More advice on ground covers: Keep these areas small. Avoid very large areas of ground cover; for large areas, use lawn.

To get a weed-free area for your ground cover, first go over the entire site with a hand-pump sprayer and some Roundup herbicide. Roundup is expensive, and the less expensive jugs of it are less concentrated. Buy the 25 percent concentrate spray. It costs a little bit more but is twice as effective.

Spray all the grass and weeds in the area thoroughly. If it's windy, wait. Roundup is a nonselective weed killer and will kill any plant it lands on. No point in killing off your shrubs and flowers!

Tips Tips Tips Tips

### *Insider's Tip*

Herbicides work better if it's a hot, sunny day when you spray. The effectiveness of any herbicide is improved if you add a few tablespoons of dish soap to the spray mix. The soap helps the herbicide stick to the leaves better.

Once you've sprayed the entire area, wait another week and then go back over it and respray anything that's still green. Some weeds, such as Bermuda grass, are very hard to kill.

When the weeds and grasses are all dead, then spread some high-nitrogen fertilizer, such as ammonium sulfate, over the entire area, using ten pounds of fertilizer for every five hundred square feet. Then sprinkle the area well, wait a day, and sprinkle it all over again. Now take a shovel and dig small holes in every spot where you intend to plant a ground cover plant. Sprinkle the whole area every other day for the next several weeks. At the end of this time, new weeds will have sprouted. Spray them all over again with the weed killer, wait a few days—and you're finally ready to plant.

This process probably sounds way too long and drawn out, but it will save you a lot of hassle in the long run. Nothing looks shabbier than a ground cover that is full of weeds. And once the ground cover plants are in place and starting to grow in, weeding becomes very difficult. You're better off doing it right in the first place.

## MULCH AND GROUND COVERS

The areas between ground cover plants should be covered with some kind of mulch. Simply put, mulch is anything used to cover the ground. Small fir bark, which you can buy in large sacks inexpensively, makes good mulch for the area between the plants.

You need only put enough of the bark down to cover the soil. Another product that works pretty well is woven horticultural-grade poly ground covering material. You then cut slits in the woven material, plant your plants through it, and then cover anything showing with small bark mulch. The weave is quite tight with this material, and weeds will have a hard time growing up through it. Because it's porous, however, water can pass right through.

### *Potential Pitfall*

Do not mulch with sheets of black or clear plastic! I see people doing this all the time. They then cover the plastic with bark. With the first rain, the bark slides around on the plastic, leaving ugly bare spots. Rainwater can't go through this plastic, either, and eventually the whole thing becomes one big mess. In a few years, the plastic gets brittle and starts to rip and tear and up come the weeds through the mess. Spend a few extra dollars and use the woven material.

With perennial, herbaceous-type plants, you can go ahead and plant them close so that they'll fill in sooner. But woody ground cover plants such as juniper, cotoneaster, Natal plum, bougainvillea, landscape roses, and manzanita will not look good if you have to prune the edges. To avoid this, do not plant any of them too close to any walkway. If a plant has an ultimate spread of four feet, then do not plant it closer than two feet to any sidewalk! Also, you don't want these woody plants growing up on top of each other, so space them far enough apart.

## Two Ground Covers to Avoid Like the Plague

- **Coyote brush (*Baccharis* spp.)** This low-growing shrub is often recommended as a ground cover for large, dry areas. It has two main drawbacks: First, it's short lived and will start to die off in patches after a few years. Also, it's a ragweed relative—and all the coyote brush sold is the male, highly allergenic kind. Don't waste your time with it!

- **Ivy, English ivy, or Algerian ivy (*Hedera* spp.)** Don't use it. Ivy has a habit of spreading far beyond where you intended it to stay. It also has a bad habit of climbing up trees and, if left unchecked, will eventually kill the tree. Ivy, especially the mild-winter-area, big-leafed Algerian ivy, often changes form to what's called "mature ivy" after quite a few years. This has a more rounded leaf and also blooms, producing allergenic pollen. I'd pass on the ivy.

## Recommended Ground Covers

- **Carpet bugle *(Ajuga reptans).*** Often useful as a low-pollen ground cover for smaller areas, carpet bugle is much easier to establish where summer rains are common. In some Southern states, it does escape into the woods and naturalize. In the drier West, it will grow all right but only if watered regularly. *Ajuga* will grow in sun or shade but often does best in shady or semishady spots. It's low growing and has small blue flowers and dark, bronzy green leaves. *Ajuga* looks especially good growing around a tree that is planted in the lawn.

- **Red apple ice plant *(Aptenia cordata).*** Best used in mild-winter areas, it has very little pollen and grows easy and fast. Red apple spreads quickly and can be planted from unrooted cuttings. It will grow in full sun or in the shade. Once established, it's quite drought tolerant. Red apple is good for steep hillsides and it is very nonflammable—also a plus. It doesn't take any foot traffic, though, so if you'll need to walk through this ground cover, put down some stepping-stones.

- **Manzanita (*Arctostaphylos* spp.)** has much going for it. Manzanita is low allergy, drought tolerant, and longer lived than many other ground-cover-type shrubs. There are many different species used for ground covers, and they vary greatly in winter hardiness. The most winter hardy of all of them, *A. uva-ursi,* bearberry, will grow in all parts of the country. Manzanita as ground cover appears to be gaining in popularity—a trend certainly to be encouraged. This is one plant that will work okay for larger areas, especially on slopes. It needs little water in summer. Before you set out the manzanita plants, be sure to find out what their ultimate spread will be; this will be different with each species and each cultivar sold. Set out these plants so that at maturity they will just touch each other; if they're too close, they'll eventually be too crowded.

- **Buffalo grass *(Buchloe dactyloides)*** can make a good allergy-free ground cover if a female cultivar is used. Now, you might say, didn't he recommend this stuff as a lawn grass? Well, yes, I did. Buffalo grass can be used as a lawn that you mow, and it can also be used as a ground cover that you never mow. Just because a plant is a grass doesn't automatically mean that it's only for lawns and can't be used as ground cover material. Actually, there are a number of no-mow grasses that are commonly used as ground covers. Of these, I like buffalo grass best.

  As of this writing, the best buffalo grass cultivar is one called 'Legacy'. 'Legacy' is blue-green in color, stays very low—often well under six inches tall—and is very drought tolerant once established. 'Legacy' grows best in full sun but tolerates shade better than the older types of buffalo grass. It can also be used as a no-mow ground cover for hillsides.

  The main drawback to all kinds of buffalo grass is that they are summer grasses and turn completely dormant in winter. This makes them less useful in zone 10, but they can be mowed short and overseeded with winter annual grasses if needed. Also, in my own tests I have found that occasionally 'Legacy' will throw up some male pollen-bearing flower heads. This pollen is sterile, but it's nonetheless undesirable. When I mowed the 'Legacy' once a month, it produced very few pollen flowers. I have also been testing a female clone called '609', which never produced any male flowers at all.

'Legacy' or '609' can be bought as either plugs or sod. Plugs planted six inches apart will take about a season to fill in totally. Buffalo grass grown from seed will contain many male plants and is not recommend.

- **Bird's-foot trefoil *(Lotus corniculatus).*** Hardy in all areas, bird's-foot trefoil is a clover relative—a legume with small, bright yellow flowers. It makes a fairly decent ground cover for sunny areas and is useful for covering banks. After the flowers fall off, they are followed by little seedpods that look much like a small bird's foot, hence the name. Trefoil seed can be bought at a farm supply store; it's not very expensive. Scatter the small seed rather thickly, using twenty-five pounds to cover an area of five hundred square feet. Sprinkle on fertilizer, ammonium sulfate, at twenty pounds per five hundred square feet, and then sprinkle on a very thin layer of steer manure. Use just enough manure to cover the seed, no more.

  Keep the area well sprinkled for the first two weeks and you'll get a thick stand of trefoil. Plant in springtime, if possible, and mow it all once late in summer with a power mower. Set the mower high—three to three and a half inches. In subsequent years, you can mow your trefoil ground cover about once every six weeks, or you can just let it grow. Trefoil is fairly drought tolerant once it is well established. Once a year, give this ground cover some fertilizer that's high in phosphorus and low in nitrogen.

- **Bishop's weed (*Aegopodium podagraria* 'Variegatum')** is a variegated, vigorous ground cover in dry shady areas. It'll grow well in poor soil, including clay. By the end of hot, dry summers, the foliage may look ragged. If this happens, mow it down to about three inches and water it deeply to encourage new growth.

- **Blue star creeper *(Laurentia fluviatilis).*** This little, low-growing ground cover has blue flowers in early spring and throughout the summer in sunny or partially shaded areas—it can be used just about anywhere in the country. It's attractive but can be fussy. Needs regular watering. No mowing needed. Not for large areas.

- **Bougainvillea 'Crimson Jewel'** is a small, bushy bougainvillea that is useful as a ground cover in mild-winter areas in full-sun spots. This thorny plant will spread to create a cover about two feet high. Each plant will eventually spread to about five feet wide. It can look spectacular on hillsides. Do not set these plants too close to each other. Also, don't plant any plants too close to a sidewalk. Consider the ultimate spread of the plants, and keep in mind that you won't want to have to prune this one when it reaches the pavement. Plants will look much better if not pruned.
- **Campanula *(C. poscharskyana).*** This is a cute, easy-to-grow, tough little plant that has attractive blue flowers. In most places, it can be used in full sun, but in warmer climates it should only be used in partial shade. Not for large areas, it looks good growing around a lawn tree. No foot traffic.
- **Caraway-scented thyme *(Thymus herba-barona).*** All climates. Plant all thymes six to eight inches apart. Mow once each summer. Rose-pink flowers cover the plants in early summer and attract bees.
- **Natal plum *(Carissa grandiflora)*** is another good, low-growing, attractive ground-cover-like shrub for mild-winter areas. It is generally easy to grow, long lasting, and produces almost no pollen. It does, however, have sharp thorns. Certain cultivars stay lower than others. Use the variety called 'Green Carpet', because it will stay low and will spread. Set plants out four feet apart and mulch well. The sap from these plants can cause skin rash, so wear gloves if pruning it. Also, don't set out any of these plants too close to a walkway; you don't want to have to prune the edges.
- **Cotoneaster *(C. dammeri).*** This is the lowest-growing, ground-hugging cotoneaster, and it's by far the best one to

use for a ground cover. It needs decent drainage to grow well, but it'll take almost any soil type. It can be an extremely attractive ground cover when grown right. Masses of bright white flowers are followed by thousands of shiny, red fruits. Set plats out three feet apart and keep them mulched and well watered the first season. Drought resistant when established. A very fine ground cover, it's also effective on steep slopes.

- **Dichondra *(D. micrantha).*** Dichondra makes a nice, very low-growing, low-allergy ground cover or lawn substitute. It does take regular watering, weeding, and fertilizing to maintain it, though. Dichondra will grow in sun or shade but will be much lower in full sun. It's better for smaller areas and unsuitable as a ground cover for hillsides or any large areas.
- **Purple wintercreeper (*Euonymus fortunei* 'Coloratus').** A useful, tough, attractive ground cover that grows thick and stays low, at six inches. Wintercreeper does not bloom, is pollen-free, and is easy to grow in full sun or light shade. It can also be used on banks. Easy to grow from cuttings. Set plants out one foot apart and mulch between them. One of the better ground cover choices.
- **Garden chamomile *(Chamaemelum nobile).*** All climates. Plant chamomile from flats, six to eight inches apart. It can be combined to good effect with O'Connor's legume. Mow the two ground covers to two inches in spring, summer, and fall. Chamomile needs good drainage to flourish.
- **Blue-flowered ornamental comfrey (*Symphytum grandiflorum* 'Hidcote Blue').** 'Hidcote Blue' is an early-spring-flowering perennial with numerous clear blue nodding flowers. Any soil type will work; it forms a weed-resistant cover of deep green foliage.
- **Ice plant *(Lampranthus spectabilis)*** does especially well along the West Coast. This species has small pink or red flowers in profusion when grown in full sun. Very drought tolerant, it's easy to grow and stays low and thick. It won't

take foot traffic but is darn near fireproof, and many people like to use it around their houses in high-fire-danger areas. Easy to grow from unrooted cuttings, stuck directly where they are to grow.

- **Juniper (*Juniperus* spp.).** There are some very useful low-growing, pollen-free female cultivars of juniper, and some species are hardy in almost all zones. 'Bar Harbor', 'Icee Blue', and 'Glenmore' are three very low-growing female cultivars of *J. horizontalis* that are useful, too.
- **Lippia *(Phyla nodiflora)*** works well in all parts of the country. It creeps and spreads to form a sturdy low mat of gray-green leaves. Tiny lilac-colored flowers bloom from spring through fall. The flowers attract a few bees. It'll go dormant in winter in cold areas. Space plants six to eight inches apart. Mow once or twice a year as needed. Will take some light foot traffic.
- **Mother-of-thyme *(Thymus praecox* subsp. *arcticus)*.** All parts of the country. Mother-of-thyme grows two to six inches tall with purple and white flowers; mow to two inches in July and then fertilize. It attracts bees when blooming.
- **O'Connor's legume *(Trifolium fragiferum)*.** Plant from seed in fall and mow to two inches the following May, July, and August. Will attract bees in summer.
- **Parrot's-beak *(Lotus berthelotii)*.** This plant is related to bird's-foot trefoil but looks much different. The tiny leaves are gray, and the flowers are brilliant red. Parrot's-beak needs to be grown in full sun and will not take overwatering. Very drought tolerant when established, and well suited for use in hot, dry areas. Set plants out eighteen inches apart and shear them back hard once each spring before the new growth starts.
- **Scotch moss *(Sagina subulata)* and the quite similar Irish moss *(Arenaria verna)*.** Both will grow in all zones, although they won't thrive in the desert. Good for planting between stepping-stones. These can form compact, mosslike masses

of slender leaves on small stems. They grow best in good, well-drained soil. Set out plants from flats or six-packs, four to six inches apart. Mowing usually isn't needed.

- **Star jasmine *(Trachelospermum jasminoides).*** Once established, star jasmine is tough and long lasting. Keep this one to small areas, though; the sweet smell of the masses of white flowers can make some people ill. Not for the perfume sensitive!
- **'Red Nancy' (*Lamium maculatum* 'Red Nancy')** is tough and fast growing. Use in shady or semishady spots; it's good under trees. Tolerant of a wide range of soils and moisture levels. The white-edged leaves light up dark garden spots.
- **Saint-John's-wort *(Hypericum calycinum).*** A useful plant for covering ground in small to medium-size areas. Saint-John's-wort will grow in shade or sun. It looks good around the base of a lawn tree. Bright yellow flowers on tough plants, but these will be several feet tall and won't take any foot traffic. Mow to four inches tall once a season.
- **Veronica *(V. repens).*** Also called speedwell, this is a four-inch-tall, low-growing ground cover plant with pale blue flowers and little leaves. Not suited to especially hot, dry areas, it is not drought tolerant and needs plenty of water in summer. It's best for small areas and does well under a lawn tree.
- **Vinca vine or big-leafed periwinkle *(Vinca major).*** Vinca will grow in shade or sun and is long lived, hardy, and easy to grow; blue flowers. Good for covering banks too steep to mow. Plant from flats, six to twelve inches apart. Not cold hardy in Northern areas. It needs some irrigation in heat of summer.
- **Vinca vine or little periwinkle *(Vinca minor).*** *Vinca minor* is slower growing than *V. major;* it's also much more cold hardy, stays lower and neater, and has nice blue flowers. Good around the base of trees. Plant *V. minor* somewhat closer than *V. major.*

- **Wild strawberry *(Fragaria chiloensis).*** Cold hardy and useful in northern areas. Will grow well in full sun or in partial shade. Does not take foot traffic well, but it's a handsome ground cover, with small white flowers. Not for large areas. Grows especially well on sandy soils.
- **Wild mock strawberry *(Fragaria indica, Duchesnea indica)*** is hardy in all parts of the country. This species of wild strawberry will grow in almost any soil type. Plants have strawberry-like leaves, white flowers, and pretty red fruits that are not edible. Good under trees.
- **Woolly yarrow *(Achillea tomentosa)*** will grow in all climates. Plant six inches apart; mow in March and July to a height of two or three inches. Fuzzy and attractive. No foot traffic!

# Appendixes

## Appendix A
### *Grasses Compared and Rated*

**RESISTANCE TO DISEASE**

| | |
|---|---|
| Highest | Tall fescue grass |
| | Zoysia grass |
| | Bahia grass |
| | Improved Bermuda grass from seed |
| | Bahia grasses |
| | Common Bermuda grass |
| | Saint Augustine grass |
| | Meadow fescues |
| | Tufted hair grass |
| | Red fescue grass |
| | Hard fescue grass |
| | Perennial ryegrass |
| | Big bluestem |
| | Buffalo grass |
| | Kentucky bluegrass |
| | Carpet grass |

| | |
|---|---|
| | Colonial bent grass |
| | Dichondra |
| Lowest | Creeping bent grass |

***RESISTANCE TO WEAR***

| | |
|---|---|
| Highest | Zoysia hybrids from sod or plugs |
| | Seeded zoysia |
| | Hybrid seeded Bermuda grasses |
| | Improved Bermuda grasses from sod |
| | Bahia grasses |
| | Tall fescue mixes |
| | Kentucky bluegrass |
| | Red fescue blends |
| | Saint Augustine grass |
| | Buffalo grass |
| | Big bluestem grass |
| | Colonial bent grass |
| | Creeping bent grass |
| Lowest | Dichondra |

***RECOVERY RATES FROM SEVERE INJURY CAUSED BY HEAVY FOOT TRAFFIC***

| | |
|---|---|
| Best | Hybrid seeded Bermuda grasses |
| | Hybrid Bermuda grass from sod |
| | Improved Bermuda grass |
| | Common Bermuda grass |
| | Saint Augustine grass |

| | |
|---|---|
| | Bahia grass |
| | Buffalo grass |
| | Creeping bent grass |
| | Kentucky bluegrass |
| | Colonial bent grass |
| | Big bluestem grass |
| | Blue grama grass |
| | Dichondra |
| | Sheep fescues |
| | Red fescues |
| | Meadow fescues |
| | Tall fescues |
| | Carpet grass |
| | Perennial ryegrass |
| Least | Annual ryegrass |

***SHADE TOLERANCE***

| | |
|---|---|
| Most | Red fescues |
| | Zoysia grass |
| | Bahia grass |
| | Saint Augustine grass |
| | Dichondra |
| | Colonial bent grass |
| | Carpet grass |
| | Tall fescue mixes |
| | Creeping bent grasses |

| | |
|---|---|
| | Meadow fescues |
| | Kentucky bluegrass |
| | Perennial ryegrass |
| | Annual ryegrass |
| | Buffalo grass |
| | Hybrid seeded Bermuda grasses |
| | Hybrid Bermuda grass from sod |
| | Seashore paspalum |
| | Improved Bermuda grass |
| | Big bluestem grass |
| | Little bluestem grass |
| | Blue grama grass |
| Least | Common Bermuda grass |

### *HEAVY CLAY SOIL TOLERANCE*

| | |
|---|---|
| Highest | Tall fescue mixes |
| | Hybrid Bermuda grass from seed |
| | Hybrid Bermuda grass from sod |
| | Improved Bermuda grass |
| | Common Bermuda grass |
| | Seashore paspalum |
| | Zoysia grasses |
| | Kentucky bluegrass |
| | Canadian bluegrass |
| | Perennial ryegrass |
| | Buffalo grass |

| | |
|---|---|
| | Meadow fescues |
| | Big bluestem grass |
| | Little bluestem grass |
| | Blue grama grass |
| | Bahia grass |
| | Saint Augustine grass |
| | Red fescue mixes |
| | Dichondra |
| | Colonial bent grass |
| | Carpet grass |
| Least | Creeping bent grasses |

***COLD WEATHER, SNOW, AND ICE TOLERANCE***

| | |
|---|---|
| Highest | Canadian bluegrass |
| | Perennial ryegrass |
| | Kentucky bluegrass |
| | Big bluestem grass |
| | Little bluestem grass |
| | Creeping bent grasses |
| | Colonial bent grass |
| | Buffalo grass |
| | Blue grama grass |
| | Red fescue |
| | Tufted hair grass |
| | Hard fescue |
| | Meadow Fescue |

| | |
|---|---|
| | Dichondra |
| | Saint Augustine grass |
| | Hybrid seeded Bermuda grasses |
| | Hybrid Bermuda grass sod |
| | Bahia grass |
| | Centipede grass |
| | Common Bermuda grass |
| | Seashore paspalum |
| Lowest | Carpet grass |

***SALTY SOIL TOLERANCE***

| | |
|---|---|
| Highest | Seashore paspalum |
| | Bahia grass |
| | Carpet grass |
| | Centipede grass |
| | Creeping bent grass |
| | Improved Bermuda grasses |
| | Zoysia hybrids from seed |
| | Zoysia hybrids from sod or plugs |
| | Buffalo grass hybrids |
| | Buffalo grass from seed |
| | Big bluestem grass |
| | Little bluestem grass |
| | Common Bermuda grass |
| | Saint Augustine grass |

| | |
|---|---|
| | Tall fescue mixes |
| | Perennial ryegrass |
| | Meadow fescue |
| | Red fescue |
| | Canadian bluegrass |
| | Kentucky bluegrass |
| | Colonial bent grass |
| Lowest | Dichondra |

***THATCH BUILDUP***

| | |
|---|---|
| Most thatch | Kikuyu grass |
| | Centipede grass |
| | Saint Augustine grass |
| | Seashore paspalum |
| | Creeping bent grass |
| | Colonial bent grass |
| | Zoysia grass |
| | Bermuda grass hybrids |
| | Common Bermuda grass |
| | Carpet grass |
| | Red fescue grass |
| | Improved Kentucky bluegrass cultivars |
| | Bahia grass |
| | Big bluestem grass |
| | Buffalo grass |

| | |
|---|---|
| | Tall fescue grass |
| | Perennial ryegrass |
| Least thatch | Dichondra |

***COMPARING KENTUCKY BLUEGRASS, BERMUDA GRASS, AND ZOYSIA GRASSES***

| | ***Bluegrass*** | ***Zoysia*** | ***Bermuda Hybrids*** |
|---|---|---|---|
| Expected life of lawn in Southern areas | 2–5 years | very long | long |
| Fertilizer needs | 4 times a year | 2 times a year | 6 times a year |
| Months needed for establishment | | | 3–4 |
| For bare feet? | excellent | rough | good |
| Lawn color | | | |
| Cold weather | fair | dormant/poor | dormant/poor |
| Cool weather | excellent | fair | fair |
| Hot weather | poor | excellent | excellent |
| Height to mow | 2–3″ | ½–1″ | ½–1.5″ |
| How often to mow? | weekly | every 2 weeks | every 5 days |
| Typical water needs (per week) | 1–2″ | 1–2″ | 1–2″ |

***COOL-SEASON LAWNS COMPARED WITH WARM-SEASON LAWNS***

| ***Cool-Season Lawn Grasses*** | | | | | |
|---|---|---|---|---|---|
| ***Type*** | ***Texture*** | ***Maintenance*** | ***Main Uses*** | ***Looks*** | ***Cost to Establish*** |
| Bent grass | fine | very high | golf putting greens | remarkable | high |

| | | | | | |
|---|---|---|---|---|---|
| Blue-grass | medium fine | low | lawns | good | low |
| Tall fescue | medium | medium | lawns, sports | average to good | medium |
| Creeping fescues | fine | medium | lawns | good to excellent | medium |
| Annual ryegrass | fine | medium | overseeding | good | low |
| Perennial ryegrass | medium | low | lawns, sports, mixes | fair | medium |

***Warm-Season Lawn Grasses***

| *Type* | *Texture* | *Maintenance* | *Main Uses* | *Looks* | *Cost to Establish* |
|---|---|---|---|---|---|
| Bahia | coarse to medium | low | lawns, erosion control | average to good | low to medium |
| Buffalo hybrids | fine | low | lawns, no-mow areas | very good | high |
| Hybrid Bermuda | fine | medium | lawns, golf, sports | good | medium to high |
| Carpet grass | medium | low | wet areas | below average | low |
| Centipede | medium | low | lawns | below average | low |
| Saint Augustine | coarse | medium | lawns | fair | medium to high |
| Zoysia | medium fine | high | lawns | good to excellent | high |

**WARM-WINTER-AREA (SOUTHERN) GRASS SPECIES**

| *Species* | *Planting Methods* | *Uses* | *Pro* | *Con* |
|---|---|---|---|---|
| Bahia grass | seed, sod, plugs | lawns | salt-tolerant, tolerates wet soil | not cold hardy, thatch, itchy seeds |
| Blue grama | seed, plugs | lawns, no-mow slopes, wildflowers | drought tolerant | not a thick lawn |
| Buffalo grass | seed, sod, plugs | lawns, slopes, no-mow areas | drought tolerant, less mowing, less fertilizer, pollen-free cultivars | long dormancy |
| Carpet grass | stolons | low mainte-nance | tolerates wet soil, shade tolerant | ugly seed heads |
| Centipede grass | rhizomes, stolons | lawns | okay for acid soil, less mowing, slow growth | not cold hardy, thatch |
| Common Bermuda | seed | lawns | tough, easy to grow, takes low mowing, durable | allergies, thatch, invasive |
| Hybrid Bermuda | seed, sod | lawns | attractive, dur-able, pollen-free | expensive |
| Hybrid buffalo grass | sod, plugs | lawns | female cultivars pollen-free, shorter dormancy | expensive |
| Saint Augustine grass | sod, plugs, stolons | lawns | easy to grow, tough, durable | not drought tolerant |

| | | | | |
|---|---|---|---|---|
| Zoysia grass | seed, plugs, sod | lawns | salt tolerant, shade tolerant, tough, drought tolerant | long dormancy |

***FESCUE VARIETIES***

| *Variety* | *Description* | *Pro* | *Comments* |
|---|---|---|---|
| 'Aurora Gold' | medium green, fine texture | needs less care than most | Roundup (glyphosate) tolerant |
| 'Banner' | dark green, dense, fine texture | tolerates short mowing | competes well with bluegrass, fair disease resistance |
| 'Bighorn' | blue-green color | drought tolerant | thrives on neglect |
| 'Boreal' | dark green, medium texture | strong seedling vigor | good winter hardiness |
| 'Cascade' | medium green, very fine texture | seedlings vigorous | watch for leaf spot |
| 'Dawson' | medium green, fine texture | good for overseeding of Bermuda grass lawns | watch for dollar spot |
| 'Duster' | tall fescue type | not fussy, low fertility requirements | good winter hardiness |
| 'Kentucky 31' | tall fescue | tough, good for athletic fields | drought tolerant |
| 'Plantation' | top-rated tall fescue, dark green color, fine texture | drought tolerant, low mowing | easy care |
| 'Virtue' | low-growing, dwarf type | tough, low mowing | better than most in shade |

**SEEDING AND GERMINATION RATES**

| *Species of grass* | *Lbs. of seed per 1,000 Sq. Ft.* | *Days to Germinate* |
|---|---|---|
| Annual ryegrass | 8–12 | 4–9 |
| Bahia grass | 8–10 | 10–12 |
| Bermuda grass | 1–3 | 8–20 |
| Big bluestem grass | 2–3 | 3–30 |
| Blue grama grass | 1–2 | 20–50 |
| Buffalo grass | 1–3 | 8–30 |
| Carpet grass | 3–10 | 12–24 |
| Centipede grass | 4–6 | 8–15 |
| Chewings fescue | 4–5 | 7–14 |
| Colonial bent grass | ½–1 | 8–15 |
| Creeping bent grass | ½–1 | 7–10 |
| Creeping bluegrass | 2–4 | 7–8 |
| Creeping red fescue | 4–5 | 7–14 |
| Dichondra (not a true grass) | 4–6 | 10–20 |
| Hard fescue | 4–5 | 7–14 |
| Kentucky bluegrass | 2–3 | 7–30 |
| Perennial ryegrass | 10–12 | 6–14 |
| Rough bluegrass | 2–3 | 8–20 |
| Tall fescue | 8–10 | 5–12 |
| Zoysia grass | 2–4 | 12–16 |

# Appendix B

## *Fertilizers*

***COMMON ORGANIC FERTILIZERS COMPARED***

| *Fertilizer* | *% Nitrogen* | *% Phosphorus* | *% Potassium* | *Use per 1,000 Sq. Ft.* |
|---|---|---|---|---|
| Blood meal | 14 | 3 | 0.5 | 30 lbs. |
| Bonemeal | 4 | 20 | 0.5 | 50 lbs. |
| Compost | 0.5 | 0.5 | 0.5 | 200–300 lbs. |
| Composted sludge | 1 | 2 | 0 | 100+ lbs. |
| Cottonseed meal | 6 | 3 | 2 | 50 lbs. |
| Cow manure | 1.5 | 1 | 1.5 | 150 lbs. |
| Dried chicken manure | 6–7 | 2–3 | 1–2 | 50 lbs. |
| Fish emulsion | 5 | 1 | 1 | 1 gallon |
| Granite dust | 0 | 0 | 8 | 30–50 lbs. |
| Grass clippings | 2 | 1 | 0.5% | mowing |
| Mushroom compost | 1–2 | 1 | 1 | 100–200 lbs. |
| Soybean meal | 7 | 1 | 1 | 50 lbs. |
| Steer manure | 2 | 1.5 | 1.5 | 150 lbs. |
| Rock phosphate | 0 | 30 | 0 | 35 lbs. |
| Wood ashes | 0 | 1.5 | 6 | 30 lbs. |

Almost all of these fertilizers also have many other important plant macro- and micronutrients and generally come in a slow-release form.

- Mushroom compost, steer and cow manure, chicken manure, bonemeal, and blood meal may all contain considerable fungus spores. It's a very good idea to wear a face mask when spreading these.

- Cottonseed meal is high in chemical pollutants.
- Wood ashes will raise soil pH and are more effective on acidic soils.
- Steer manure has fewer weed seeds than does cow manure.
- Sludge products may be high in unhealthy heavy metals.

### NITROGEN FERTILIZATION RATES

**Actual Nitrogen Needed Per Thousand Square Feet of Lawn Per Year**

| | Low | High |
|---|---|---|
| Bahia grass | 2 | 6 |
| Bent grass | 2 | 6 |
| Bermuda grass | 3 | 8 |
| Blue grama grass | 1 | 4 |
| Bluegrass | 2 | 5 |
| Buffalo grass | 1 | 5 |
| Carpet grass | 2 | 3 |
| Centipede grass | 2 | 3 |
| Fescue/tall fescue | 2 | 4 |
| Fescue/creeping red fescue | 1 | 3 |
| Fescue/Chewings | 1 | 2 |
| Fescue/hard and sheep fescues | 1 | 2 |
| Ryegrass/annual | 2 | 4 |
| Ryegrass/perennial | 3 | 8 |
| Saint Augustine grass | 4 | 7 |
| Zoysia grass | 2 | 4 |

### LIME NEEDED TO RAISE SOIL PH

The pH scale runs from 1 through14. The number 7 is considered "neutral"; below 7, soil becomes acidic, and above 7 it becomes alkaline. Soil that is too acidic or too alkaline will not grow a good lawn. Lime, which is alkaline and supplies calcium, is used to raise the pH of acidy soils. A pH of between 6.5 and 7 is considered good for most lawns, but 6.5 is considered better than 7. Don't overlime.

Remember, a thousand square feet is a piece that is twenty feet wide by fifty feet long. Always use length times width (L x W) to figure square footage.

**Pounds of Limestone Used per 1,000 Sq. Ft.**

| pH Change Wanted | Sandy Soil | Loam | Silt Loam | Clay |
|---|---|---|---|---|
| 4 to 6.5 | 70 | 160 | 190 | 230 |
| 4.5 to 6.5 | 60 | 130 | 155 | 190 |
| 5 to 6.5 | 50 | 100 | 130 | 150 |
| 5.5 to 6.5 | 40 | 80 | 90 | 105 |
| 6.0 to 6.5 | 20 | 40 | 50 | 55 |

### SOIL SULFUR NEEDED TO RAISE PH

Soil sulfur works the opposite of soil lime. For soils (usually Western soils) that are too alkaline—whose pH is too high—adding soil sulfur will often solve a whole host of problems. Any pH over 7 is too alkaline for optimum lawn growth. A soil pH of around 6.5 is ideal for almost all lawns.

| Pounds of Soil Sulfur Used per 1,000 Sq. Ft. | | | |
|---|---|---|---|
| ***pH Change Wanted*** | ***Sandy Soils*** | ***Loam*** | ***Clay Soils*** |
| 9 to 6.5 | 70 | 80 | 100 |
| 8.5 to 6.5 | 45 | 60 | 70 |
| 8 to 6.5 | 30 | 35 | 50 |
| 7.5 to 6.5 | 15 | 20 | 25 |
| 7 to 6.5 | 3 | 5 | 8 |

# Appendix C
## *Mowing*

With all species, mowing will be more frequent when the grass is growing most actively, and less frequent when it's growing slowly. Fertilization and deep watering will usually increase the need for frequency of mowing with any species.

***BEST MOWING INTERVALS***

| ***Species of Grass*** | ***Days Between Mowings*** |
|---|---|
| Bahia grass | 3–6 |
| Bent grass | 3–7 |
| Buffalo grass | 7–30 or no-mow |
| Carpet grass | 7–14 |
| Centipede grass | 7–14 |
| Colonial bent grass | 3–7 |
| Common Bermuda | 4–10 |
| Creeping red fescue | 4–7 |
| Hybrid Bermuda | 3–7 |
| Kentucky bluegrass | 5–7 |
| Perennial ryegrass | 7–9 |
| Seashore paspalum | 4–7 |
| Saint Augustine grass | 4–7 |
| Tall fescue | 7–14 |
| Zoysia grass | 7–10 |

## BEST MOWING HEIGHTS

With all lawn grasses, it's a good idea to mow a bit higher in the heat of summer. Mowing too low during periods of intense summer heat is frequently why so many lawns that were once attractive, now are not.

| | Optimum Height in Inches | | | |
|---|---|---|---|---|
| **Species** | **Spring** | **Summer** | **Fall** | **Winter** |
| Annual ryegrass | 3 | dormant | 3 | 3–4 |
| Bahia grass | 1½–3 | 2–3 | 3 | dormant |
| Bermuda grass, common | 1–3 | ½–2 | 1½–2½ | dormant |
| Buffalo grass | 2–no-mow | 1–4 | 2–no-mow | dormant |
| Carpet grass | 2–3 | 1–2 | 2–3 | dormant |
| Centipede grass | 2–3 | 1–2 | 2–3 | dormant |
| Colonial bent grass | ½–1 | ½–1 | ½–1 | ½–1 |
| Creeping bent grass | ⅓–1 | ⅓–¾ | ½–1 | ½–1 |
| Creeping red fescue | 1–2 | 2–3 | 2–3 | 2 |
| Dichondra | 1–2 | ½–1 | 1–2 | 1–2 |
| Kentucky bluegrass | 1½–2 | 2–3 | 2–3 | 3 |
| Perennial ryegrass | 2–3 | 2–3 | 2–3 | 3–4 |
| Seashore paspalum | ½–2 | ½–2½ | ½–2 | 1–2 |
| Saint Augustine grass | 2½–3 | 3–4 | 3 | 3 |
| Tall fescue | 2–3 | 3–4 | 2–3 | 3 |
| Zoysia grass | ½–1½ | 1–2½ | 1–2 | dormant |

# Appendix D

## *Twenty-Five Recommended Trees for Your Lawn*

- **Red maple 'Autumn Glory'** is a large, rounded, handsome female, pollen-free tree that loses its leaves in fall; easy to grow in bluegrass lawns. Great fall color.
- **Red maple 'October Glory'** is a female, pollen-free tree that does especially well in lawns and does not cast a deep lawn-killing shade.
- **Red maple 'Bowhall' (*Acer rubrum* 'Bowhall')** is an attractive, pollen-free deciduous female tree with excellent fall color. It grows narrowly upright and is a good lawn tree for smaller yards. The shade is not dense.
- **Crab apple 'Molten Lava' (*Malus* spp.).** A smaller, very pretty, flowering crab apple tree, to ten feet tall, with great flowers in spring and small red fruits in fall. Does fine in well-drained lawns, and is an especially disease-resistant tree.
- **Crab apple 'Dolgo' (*Malus* 'Dolgo').** Pink buds open to fragrant, white flowers in late spring. Glossy, dark green foliage turns yellow in fall and has good disease resistance. Large, almost fluorescent, bright red fruit ripening in early summer is excellent for crab apple jelly. A hardy tree with a spreading, upright, and open habit. Does well in bluegrass lawns.
- **Crab apple 'Red Splendour' (*Malus* spp.).** Greenish red leaves with rose-pink flowers. Small red fruit stays on the tree well into winter. Good resistance to disease. An upright-growing smaller crab apple tree, good in lawns.
- **Crab apple 'Snowcloud'** produces profuse double white flowers, mostly pollen-free and fruitless. Bright green leaves on a smaller tree—to twenty feet tall.
- **Crab apple 'Sugar Tyme'** produces pale pink buds that open to fragrant, showy white blossoms, which cover the tree in spring. A bounty of small, persistent, bright red fruits are

produced in fall and attract birds. This vigorous tree has crisp, dark green leaves and an upright, oval habit. One of the most disease-resistant flowering crab apples.

- **Flowering plum (*Prunus* spp.)** is a pretty, easy-to-grow tree. It loses its leaves in fall and flowers in spring. A fast grower, it likes frequent irrigating, as in a lawn. The shade is not dense.
- **Apricot trees (*Prunus* spp.)** are attractive, lose their leaves in fall, and are easy to grow in Western areas. The blossoms smell great, and the fruit is good. They should be pruned so they're not difficult to mow under. Does not cast a dense shade. Good fall color, too.
- **Fuyu persimmon tree *(Diospyros kaki)*** is slow growing, produces very attractive bark and leaves, and sports beautiful, sweet, and excellent fruit. The tree is female and pollen-free. Incredible fall color.
- **Pineapple guava tree *(Feijoa sellowiana)*** is a small evergreen tree. Best grown as a multitrunked tree, to eighteen feet tall, gray-green attractive leaves, white-red flowers, and sweet green fruit. With age, the tree becomes more and more attractive, the bark ever more interesting.
- **Honey locust tree *(Gleditsia triacanthos)*** is a nice, medium-size shade tree. It loses its leaves in fall, grows well in lawns, and does not cast a deep grass-killing type of shade.
- **Variegated box elder (*Acer negundo* 'Variegata')** is an attractive, smaller three-leafed maple tree with beautiful variegated green-and-white leaves. Deciduous, female, and pollen-free, it's easy to grow and does well in lawns. The shade is not dense.
- **Fringe tree *(Chionanthus virginicus)*.** If you can find one that has small black fruits on it, then it's a pollen-free female—a much-desired lawn tree. The roots go down and stay down; the foliage is very attractive, with leaves lost in

winter. Attractive, lightly fragrant bright white flowers. Grows well in lawns. The shade is not dense.

- **Sourwood tree *(Nyssa sylvatica)*** is a small to medium-size lawn tree, deciduous, excellent fall color. Female sourwood trees are pollen-free; look for the exceptional cultivar called 'Miss Scarlet', which has terrific red fall color, attractive small ornamental blue fruit, and no pollen. These trees thrive in acidic soils and will not do well with alkaline soil.
- **Japanese raisin tree *(Hovenia dulcis).*** The female trees have small, sweet, raisinlike fruit and are pollen-free. Raisin trees have beautiful leaves, are deciduous, grow well in lawns, and do not cast a deep shade.
- **Hardy rubber tree *(Eucommia ulmoides)*** is a large shade tree that does not cast deep shade. If you can find a fruiting tree, it will be female and pollen-free, too. Roots stay down, and tree grows well in bluegrass lawns.
- **Pomegranate tree *(Punica granatum)*** makes a beautiful, small lawn tree if grown as either a single- or three-trunked tree. Pomegranate thrives where summer heat is high. It loses its leaves in fall after bright yellow fall color. The shade is not dense. Attractive orange flowers and red fruit. It grows well in a fescue, Bermuda grass, or Saint Augustine lawn.
- **Bougainvillea.** Not normally thought of as a tree at all, a bougainvillea can easily be trained into an unusual and quite beautiful small lawn tree. The best way to do this is to pound a strong eight-foot metal stake several feet into the ground, and then plant three one-gallon bougainvillea plants around the stake. Trim the plants back to one or two of the longest, most vigorous branches, and weave these up the stake. It takes about a year to develop this into a tree form. Keep the trunk leaf-free and shear the top several times a year for a lollipop shape. The best cultivars for this are 'San Diego Red' and the variegated 'Raspberry Ice' bougainvillea. There are some fantastic bougainvillea trees at Disneyland.

- **Quaking aspen 'Pendula'** ***(Populus tremuloides*** **'Pendula')** grows in all climates. This is a medium-size, pollen-free, female weeping aspen tree, very attractive, good fall color, easy to grow, and fast growing. It doesn't cast a deep shade and grows well in most lawns.
- **Black poplar, 'Theves' poplar (*Populus nigra* 'Afghanica', *P. n.* 'Thevestina')** is an attractive, medium-size, tall, narrowly upright shade tree, winter hardy in all parts of the country. 'Theves' poplar is female, pollen-free, and has bright yellow fall color. It's good in lawns where a narrow tree is needed.
- **'Noreaster' poplar (*Populus* 'Noreaster')** is a good, larger shade tree for lawns. 'Noreaster' is a sterile female tree—no seeds and no pollen. It does well in most bluegrass lawns and is winter hardy in even the coldest areas.
- **Japanese paper mulberry trees** ***(Broussonetia kazinoki)*** are separate sexed; if you can find a fruiting tree, it will be pollen-free. These do not cast deep shade like most of the other mulberry species and will thrive in lawns in most cool areas.
- **Paperbark maple** ***(Acer griseum)*** is a small to medium-size maple tree that has exceptionally beautiful bark and is totally handsome at all times of year. Paperbark maple doesn't cast a deep shade, and lawn will grow quite well underneath it. It's best in soils that are well drained and slightly acidic.

# Resources

## Links

Good lawn advice site, UK:
http://www.perfectlawns.co.uk/general-lawn-advice.html

Good integrated pest management advice from the University of California: http://www.ipm.ucdavis.edu/

More good IPM advice from the site of the Integrated Pest Management Practitioners Association:
http://www.efn.org/~ipmpa/

Great lawn advice: http://www.americanlawns.com

Owls: http://www.owlpages.com/owlboxes.html

Excellent site for lawn advice or for hiring a pro:
http://www.American-Lawns.com

Soil testing links:
http://www.css.cornell.edu/soiltest/soil_testing/index.asp

Good place for excellent nursery spades for edging lawns:
http://www.surelocedging.com/nursery_series_spades.htm

Another link for good spades:
http://www.bamboogardener.com/tools.html

UK site for fine hand edgers:
http://www.justoffbase-tools.co.uk

Good UK site for hard-to-find handtools:
http://www.gonegardening.com/gg_shop/

### Organic Lawns

Healthy Lawns is a very good Canadian government lawn site. The goal of the Healthy Lawns Strategy is to help reduce Canadians' reliance on pesticide use for lawn care through the application of integrated pest management principles, with particular emphasis on pest prevention, use of reduced risk products, and application of pesticides only when necessary: http://www.healthylawns.net/english/index-e.html

LessLawn.com is a site devoted to ground covers and other alternative lawn substitutes. Quite interesting, thought provoking, and informative. Many good tips on organic methods also: http://www.lesslawn.com/articles/article1050.html

The Ohio State University site is worth looking at on fertilizers: http://ohioline.osu.edu/hyg-fact/4000/4006.html

University of Minnesota site, lawn fertilizers: http://www.extension.umn.edu/distribution/horticulture/DG6551.html

Washington State University site with many good articles: http://spokane-county.wsu.edu/spokane/eastside/lawns%20&%20groundcovers/lawns&.htm

### Commercial Sites

Good UK site: http://www.perfectlawns.co.uk/

Q Lawns, a UK sod source: http://www.qlawns.co.uk/

The National Turfgrass Evaluation Program has lots of hard data on individual grass sod cultivars and seed cultivars, many by state or area. If you are very picky and want to know, for example, which exact type of tall fescue was the greenest in Arizona tests, or Mississippi, here's the site: http://www.ntep.org/

Very extensive, helpful UK site for lawns and garden links and advice: http://www.gardenlinks.ndo.co.uk/lawns.htm

DoItYourself.com is one of the best commercial sites, with lots of good info: http://doityourself.com/lawn/

Good commercial site for lawn sprinklers, repairs, advice: http://www.progardenbiz.com/currentissue/Feature1.html

For the Carolinas: http://www.turffiles.ncsu.edu/pubs/ag69.html

## Recommended Books

Clark, David, and Elizabeth Hogan, editors, *Sunset Western Garden Book*. Menlo Park, California: Lane Publishing Company, 1986. For the Western United States, this is a very useful all-around good gardening book.

Green, Douglas, *The Everything Lawn Care Book*. Holbrook, Massachusetts: Adams Media Corp., 2001. A very good book on growing lawns, especially from an organic approach.

Greenlee, John. *The Encyclopedia of Ornamental Grasses*. Emmaus, Pennsylvania: Rodale Press, 2000. One of the very best books on ornamental grasses.

Jacobsen, Arthur Lee. *North American Landscape Trees*. Berkeley, California: Ten Speed Press, 1996. One of the very best books on trees, especially lawn trees. Great attention to detail.

Ogren, Thomas Leo. *Allergy-Free Gardening*. Berkeley, California: Ten Speed Press, 2000. The most extensive book on creating allergy-free yards, gardens, and landscapes. Three-thousand-plus landscape plants are individually allergy-ranked on a scale of 1 through 10 (OPALS), where 1 is least allergenic and 10 is most.

Peattie, Donald Culross. *A Natural History of Trees of Eastern and Central North America,* and *A Natural History of Western Trees*. Boston: Houghton Mifflin Company, 1991. These are two of my favorite books on trees, extremely readable and packed with interesting information.

Taylor, Norman. *Taylor's Encyclopedia of Gardening*. Cambridge, Massachusetts: Houghton Mifflin Company, 1948. This old but wonderful book is still one of my all-time favorites, and a book I refer to often.

# Lawn Glossary

**Ammonium sulfate:** A white, granular chemical lawn fertilizer, 21–0–0, 21 percent nitrogen, containing considerable sulfur. Ammonium sulfate is inexpensive, fast acting, and, because of its high sulfur content, has an acidifying effect on the soil pH.

**Annual:** A plant that lives for only one season and then dies.

**Asexual:** Without sex. Asexual propagation of plants does not include using seeds but would include using sod, plugs, division, and sprigs.

**Biennial:** A plant that lives for two seasons and then dies. Most biennial plants flower only in their second season.

**Broadleaf weeds:** Those weeds that are not types of grasses. Crabgrass is not a broadleaf weed, but dandelions, clovers, and plantains are.

**Calcium nitrate:** A white, chemical, granular lawn fertilizer that is high in nitrogen, fast acting, and supplies considerable calcium to the lawn. Calcium nitrate has its nitrogen in a nitrate form, which makes it faster acting than ammonium fertilizers, and also makes it less acidic. This is a superior nitrogen fertilizer for colder weather.

**Contact herbicide:** A weed killer that only kills the parts of the plants it actually contacts. It might not kill off their roots.

**Cool-season grasses:** Grasses that grow best where summers are cool. Cool-season grasses can be grown in hot-summer areas, but only with much additional watering, and often with difficulty. In warm-summer areas, cool-season grasses can be used in seed mixes. Common cool-season grasses include all the bluegrasses, all types of ryegrass, all fescues, and all bent grasses.

**Crown:** A cluster of vegetative buds. Most winter-hardy plants form crowns at or just below the soil line. If the top of the plant is killed off from cold or frost, the plant itself can regrow from the buds in the crown. With perennial flowers, a mulch is a good way to protect the crown from extreme cold.

**Cultivar:** A cultivated variety.

**Dicots:** Short for "dicotyledon," these are plants that emerge from the soil as seedlings with two seed leaves (cotyledons). All broadleaf weeds are dicots, as are plants such as tomatoes, beans, oak trees, and roses. Grasses are not dicots.

**Dioecious:** *Di* is Latin for "two" and *oecious* is Latin for "houses," thus *dioecious* means "two houses." A dioecious plant is one that is separate sexed. One plant will be all male, and another will be all female. With all dioecious plants, only the males produce any pollen. Buffalo grass, salt grass and Texas bluegrass are all dioecious, separate-sexed species.

**Dormant:** The condition that a warm-season grass is in during wintertime. When a plant is dormant, it's still alive but not actively growing. Dormant grasses often turn brown but their roots are still alive, and sometimes even growing slowly while dormant.

**Fungicide:** A substance, usually a chemical, used to kill fungus.

**Genus:** Singular of *genera*. The genus is the first part of a plant or animal's scientific name. *Genus* is Latin for "group."

**Herb, herbaceous:** A plant without woody stems. A bluegrass plant is an herb, as is a tomato plant, but shrubs or trees are not herbs, because they grow woody stems and trunks. A juniper bush is an example of a woody plant.

**Herbicide:** Any chemical used to kill weeds.

**Lime:** A naturally occurring material, high in calcium, that's alkaline and will raise soil pH levels. It's most useful as an additive for soils that are too acidic.

**Macronutrients:** Elements that are needed in large amounts for plant growth. These include nitrogen, phosphorous, potassium, calcium, iron, and sulfur.

**Micronutrients:** Elements that are needed in small amounts for plant growth. Examples are magnesium, copper, and selenium.

**Miticide:** A chemical used to kill mites and other spider-related pests.

**Monocots:** Short for "monocotyledons," these are the grasses and grass-related plants that emerge from a seed in the ground with one first leaf. Monocots also include plants such as corn, lilies, onions, bamboo, and palm trees.

**Mulch:** Anything used to cover the soil. Mulches can be either organic (such as bark or leaves) or inorganic (like rock or gravel). Mulches keep weeds from sprouting, keep soil moisture from evaporating, and tend to keep soils in better shape. Earthworms and other beneficial soil creatures will be more plentiful under mulch than in bare soil. Good, experienced gardeners understand and use mulch.

**Naturalize:** When a domestic plant spreads from where it's planted and starts to grow on its own in the wild, it's said to naturalize. Japanese honeysuckle has naturalized throughout much of the Southeastern United States.

**Nematodes:** Tiny wireworms that live in the soil and eat the roots of plants. Nematodes can be very destructive to many kinds of plants, including lawn grasses. Interestingly, there are also predatory nematodes that kill the harmful ones. These can be bought and spread where needed, and they're quite effective. Nematodes are much more common on sandy soils than in loam or clay.

**NPK:** Nitrogen, phosphorous, and potassium. Macronutrients. These are the three main ingredients in all fertilizers. A fertilizer is said to be complete if it has some of each of these three components.

**Perennial:** Herbaceous plants that live for more than two years. Most perennials are winter hardy, and even if the tops die off in winter, the crown and roots stay alive below the soil. Peonies and tiger lilies are both perennials, as are most of our best lawn grass species.

**Pesticide:** A substance used to kill plant pests, generally insects or mites. There are chemical pesticides such as Sevin or malathion, and organic pesticides like neem oil and pyrethrum. There are also "synthetic organic" pesticides such as the pyrethrins. In general, organic pesticides are safer to use than chemical pesticides, but all pesticides should be handled and used with care.

**pH:** The scale that measures the acidity or the alkalinity of the soil. The pH scale runs from 1 through 14, and number 7 is considered neutral. Most lawn grasses grow best at pH levels somewhere from 6.5 to 7.

**Plugs:** Small pieces of sod, with soil usually attached to the roots, used to start lawns of improved cultivar types that will then spread and fill in to become a full lawn. Plugs are usually planted about six inches apart.

**Postemergent herbicides:** Chemical weed killers used to kill weeds that have already sprouted.

**Preemergent herbicides:** Chemical weed killers used to kill weed seed that is in the ground, before the seed sprouts and grows.

**Propagation:** Starting new plants. There are many kinds of plant propagation, including seed, bulbs, tubers, rhizomes, budding, air layering, tissue culture, grafting, and rooting from cuttings.

**Rhizomes:** Thick underground roots that are capable of sprouting new plants. Rhizomes are similar to runners, except that runners always run just above the ground and rhizomes usually run beneath it, typically just under the soil. Many lawn grasses spread by rhizomes.

**Rodenticide:** A poison used to kill mice, rats, ground squirrels, or gophers.

**Seedling grown:** Grown from seed, not cuttings, division, or any other asexual method.

**Sod:** Already-grown grass that you buy in rolls and install for an instant lawn. When planting sod, you prepare the soil just as you would if you were going to plant seed. Newly installed sod must be kept moist until it grows in. In addition, sod that has been delivered should never be left to sit around in the sun. When you get it, you need to get right to installing it. Sod left sitting in piles for much more than a day quickly suffocates and dies.

**Sour:** Soil described as sour is acidic soil, usually with a pH lower than 5.5.

**Species:** The species is the second part of every scientific name: *Genus species.* With the plant *Buchloe dactyloides,* buffalo grass, for instance, *dactyloides* is the species name of this grass. *Species* is Latin for "kind."

**Sprigs:** Some grasses are planted by scattering small pieces of the roots and rhizomes, called sprigs, which will then eventually grow into a new lawn. Grasses grown this way are Bermuda grass, some zoysia grass, centipede grass, and especially Saint Augustine grass. Sprigs must be kept well watered until they grow in.

**Stamens:** The male parts of the flowers. The pollen is held in the anther, which is on the tip of the stamen.

**Sticker spreader:** A mixture of a soaplike substance that is added to fungicides, pesticides, herbicides, or miticides to make them stick to plant leaves better, and thus make the spray more effective. Sticker spreaders are widely used in horticulture and agriculture and are cost effective. If you can't find any commercial sticker spreader to purchase, you can always add a few tablespoons of liquid dish soap to any kind of spray; it'll work almost as well as the real thing.

**Stolon:** A prostate grass stem, at or just below the soil surface, that produces buds that sprout and grow into new grass plants. Grasses that spread from stolons, such as many of the bluegrass species, are said to be stoloniferous.

**Sweet soil:** Any soil that is alkaline, or above a pH of 7.7. In many Western areas, you will pass the occasional Sweetwater Road. This is an indication that the soil in the area has a high, alkaline pH. Water from these areas will have a slightly sweet taste, just as water from highly acidic areas often has a somewhat sour flavor.

**Synergist:** Something that, when added to something else, enhances the effect of both. One of the more common synergists used in horticulture is sesame oil, which is added to pyrethrum and pyrethrin insecticide sprays to give them faster "knockdown" power.

**Systemic insecticide:** A chemical that will kill insects that eat plants treated with this product. With systemic insecticides, the poison is taken up through the roots and transported through the entire plant. Systemic herbicides work much the same as systemic insecticides.

**Turf, or turfgrass:** Lingo used by most grass and lawn experts. These experts never go to lawn conventions, for example, but they do go to turfgrass conventions. A turfgrass is simply a lawn grass. Recently, though, I'm hearing people speaking of turf or turfgrass when they're referring to a new kind of artificial lawn that's supposed to be superior to Astroturf. Still, almost all football and baseball players will tell you that they'd much rather play on a real grass lawn. It feels better and is safer.

**Variety:** A subdivision of a species. For example, Marion bluegrass is a variety of Kentucky bluegrass.

**Vegetative:** Growth that consists only of stems and leaves, but no flowers. Ideally, our lawns will remain in a constant vegetative state.

**Warm-season grasses:** Grasses that grow best where summers are warm or hot. Many of these grasses will go completely dormant, and brown, with the first frost in fall. Native warm-season grasses, such as buffalo grass or big bluestem grass, will tolerate cold winter temperatures. Most of the non-native warm-season lawn grasses will not tolerate extremely cold winter weather. Of the non-native warm-season grasses, zoysia grass is the most cold tolerant.

In very mild-winter areas, especially southern California, southern parts of Florida, and Hawaii, many warm-season grasses will remain green all year long if watered and fertilized regularly. Some other common warm-season grasses are Saint Augustine grass, Bahia grass, centipede grass, carpet grass, and Bermuda grass.

**Zones:** There are a number of different schemes used to delineate plant zones of hardiness. The oldest and most used is probably the old

USDA system, in which the United States is divided into ten zones of hardiness. In this system—which I've used in this book—zone 1 is the coldest, and zone 10 is the warmest. In zone 1, winter low temperatures may get to fifty degrees below zero Fahrenheit. In zone 10, wintertime temperatures rarely ever get much below forty degrees. The mildest-winter areas are Southern areas next to the coast, and in some of these zone 10 areas frost is seldom or never seen. Plants that are, for example, listed for zones 6 through 9 will winterkill in colder zones. Plants listed, as another example, for zones 5 through 8 may grow in the warmer zones of 9 and 10, but they will not be well adapted there and will not thrive. All plants we use in horticulture are to some degree zone sensitive. You'll always have better luck if you use plants well adapted to the zone in which you live.

# INDEX

## E



## F

## E



## F

## R



## S

## W



## X



## Z

# Acknowledgments

I'd like to thank my literary agent, Sheree Bykofsky, and my editor, John Aherne, for getting this book and this great new series off the ground. Thanks are in order too for the terrific copyediting work done by Laura Jorstad.

The entire process has been exceptionally professional and smooth, and working with everyone at Warner Books has been a real pleasure.

Look for the other books
in this series

## WHAT THE "EXPERTS" MAY *NOT* TELL YOU ABOUT™...

- BUILDING OR RENOVATING YOUR HOME
- BUYING A HOUSE OR APARTMENT
- CAR REPAIR